Dare

Gary Leboff

Dare

Take Your Life On
and Win

RICHARD

ENJOYED OUR CHAT AT

THE AM - SEE YOU IN UK

I HOPE

**HODDER
MOBIUS**

First published in Great Britain in 2006 by Hodder & Stoughton
A division of Hodder Headline

This paperback edition published in 2007

The right of Gary Leboff to be identified as the Author of the Work
has been asserted by him in accordance with the Copyright,
Designs and Patents Act 1988.

A Mobius paperback

1

A CIP catalogue record for this title is available from the British Library

ISBN 978 0 340 92395 5

Typeset in Sabon by Palimpsest Book Production Limited,
Grangemouth, Stirlingshire

Printed and bound by Clays Ltd, St Ives plc

Hodder Headline's policy is to use papers that are natural,
renewable and recyclable products and made from wood grown
in sustainable forests. The logging and manufacturing processes are
expected to conform to the environmental regulations of the
country of origin.

Hodder & Stoughton Ltd
A division of Hodder Headline
338 Euston Road
London NW1 3BH

For Jamie and Lara

ACKNOWLEDGMENTS

Funny things, acknowledgments. Unless you know the author, it would never occur to you to check you were in them. If you do know the author, the main point of looking is to see whether you've been left out.

Thanks be to those who've inspired me. To my agent David Riding (great postcards!) and my frighteningly efficient editor Helen Coyle (I bet her wardrobes are spotless). I would also have been sunk without the help, support and emotional nourishment provided by Siobhan, Judi, Paul H-P, Joel, Rodge, Gersh, Tom, Grace, Sarah and, always, my long-suffering parents.

As I get older – 47, for God's sake – I have come to hold nothing, but nothing, in higher esteem than kindness. There is a special place in my heart for those who are able to display this rare quality with complete absence of self-interest. I am thus indebted to Rozi and Neil, to Allan, Reeves, JB, Jonathan, Damian, and Alex. Most of all to Martin Perry, a coach and friend without peer.

And Dashy.

Contents

INTRODUCTION
My Story

I am about to die. This is not a dream.

Just before midday, on 12 March 1990, I walk towards the lift (or, in local parlance, 'elevator') of the St Moritz Hotel in Manhattan. I am on the fourteenth floor.

As I walk down the corridor, thinking about the flight home – this is my last day and I'll be at the airport in less than three hours – an enormous 'bang' reverberates through the hall. It seems to be coming from the direction of the lift.

A startled chambermaid appears beside me. 'I'll call down to reception,' she says. 'We'd better check what that was.' No argument from me.

Reception heard nothing, saw nothing, felt nothing. 'The lift is fine,' she assures me. I press on.

I call for the lift. I press the button for the ground floor. A moment's hesitation. The doors close. All appears to be fine but then the lift plunges straight down.

I am about to die. *I look up and see the indicator flashing through the floors – 12, 11, 10, 9. I have maybe three seconds to live.*

I should be scared but there's no fear at all. In a matter of moments, it will all be over, my body obliterated at the moment of impact. I am plunging to ground level at breakneck speed and there is not a thing I can do. I surrender and wait.

Almost there now. What a cliché – your life really does flash before you when you die. In those final seconds, I see myself as a child, as a teenager and an adult. A life. A short one. Now, it's gone.

And then it hits me. My God, how it hits me. I'm going to die – and I couldn't care less!

I was born on 26 August 1958 and spent my childhood in Edgware, a small suburb of North London. At that time, Edgware's claim to fame was as the global headquarters of Green Shield Stamps – until, that is, people got tired of filling three dozen books in return for a saucepan.

At the age of four, I was sent to a local primary school of Jewish affiliation, which was quite handy as I was Jewish. They taught all the good stuff there: how there is only one 'chosen' people (i.e. us – wasn't that an *amazing* coincidence?) and how God is jealous, angry, intolerant, demanding and (worst of all) everywhere (going to the toilet was extremely unsettling for several years). And you'd better do what he says or he'll cast your soul out with 'the other lot' (i.e. heathens, philistines and everyone but lucky old us). *All this – at four!*

What all that teaching boiled down to was that *fear is good*. Fear of sin, fear of parents, fear of teachers, fear of misfortune, fear of illness, fear of rejection, fear of affection, fear of love, fear of each other, fear of *life*. What does all this fear do? It keeps you in your place (i.e. afraid) – which is exactly where God wants you to be. He and I were going to have a few problems.

My classmates were no help. That my ears protruded more than the customary angle was all it took. I was totally isolated and treated with contempt, particularly by the boys. I was excluded from their games, from their laughter, from their friendship. The girls were better, if baffling (no change, there, as I got older). Through the eyes of other children, I saw myself as ugly.

The pain of exclusion was excruciating. Everything you have ever heard or read about bullying barely begins to scratch the surface. It is impossible to comprehend the agony of a child denied access to its peers with no power to reason why. Every time I read a newspaper report about a child or teenager who has killed themselves rather than bear the pain of being bullied for one more day, I have to resist the urge to get in the car, find the school and hold a seminar.

Home was hardly a help. I was never sure my parents liked me very much. Not that I blamed them. I didn't like myself very much. But, in the sixties, no one gave a thought to life/work balance. Dad was the Managing Director of Fobel (our surname – sort of – backwards) International plc. The company had thousands of employees across the globe and my father felt a personal responsibility towards each and every one.

Dad didn't seem to be home much. Even when he was, he always appeared to be working or talking about work or thinking about work. I remember wondering, at eight years of age, who my father was. Once or twice, I couldn't even remember what he looked like. What he lacked in physical presence, my father made up for in generosity. He was always extending a helping hand to anyone he could find. This was a trait passed down from my grandfather – a soft-hearted fitness fanatic who walked ten miles a day up and down the streets of Hove. I adored him.

Mum was enormously encouraging and unyielding in her belief in her children's abilities. She was also a strong advocate of discipline through high-pitched use of vocal cords. Mum was scary when we were little but, by the age of eleven, I was bigger than her and did what I liked. If only she'd tried whispering, I might actually have listened.

I was the eldest of three. My brother Roger (my best friend to this day) was two years younger and Laurel was born when I was five. By the age of nine, I'd gone from being a virtual outcast to the most popular boy in the class. It's amazing what being good at football can do. Education continued to be an unqualified disaster. I went to boarding school (loathsome), polytechnic (worse) and Bar School (don't get me started). I qualified as a barrister while detesting every aspect of the English Legal System. I walked out one Friday afternoon and never went back.

I spent the next four years travelling around Europe

selling computers. To this day, I've no idea how they work but it didn't stop me shifting thousands of the damn things. I soon discovered that distributors from Paris to Bratislava had no idea either, and were more interested in wining and dining at tax-deductible restaurants than debating the merits of floppy disks. Me too, which was handy.

In 1986, showing a rare interest in broadening my skills, I bought a textbook on negotiation. Although I'd lost interest by page 14, I kept going long enough to spot an advert for a pompously named organisation called the Vocational Guidance Association. You know the kind: 'Are you fulfilled in your work? Do you long to find your true vocation? Call this number and find redemption.' (I made that last bit up.)

Despite the irritating name, there was *something* about that ad. It kept prodding away in the back of my mind long after the book had been dumped in some recess of my office. It seemed to promise something I needed. I had no interest in computers beyond getting paid and was desperate to find something that would reconnect me to the gifts and purpose I knew were inside. One of the abiding beliefs I have always held – and now drum into all my life-coaching clients – is that every single person on earth has something they can do better than anyone else. I had to find mine. So, I went along to the VGA Headquarters. At the time, their offices were in Baker Street. I was soon ensconced in one of those chilly, wood-panelled, Edwardian sitting rooms that you usually find at private doctors or dentists. I had – physically – to stop myself legging it.

Dare

It was a glorious, early Spring morning. I handed over my £200 (the receptionist virtually had to prise the cheque from my cold, dead hand) and spent three hours completing a battery of verbal, numerical and special-awareness tests.

Three weeks later, I went back for the results. Naturally, I assumed I was a washout and would be told to get a job as a traffic warden, a bailiff or Prime Minister. What I could not have realised was that I was about to meet one of the most important people in my life – maybe THE most important.

Siobhan Hamilton Phillips burst into the room; a typhoon of energy, clarity and inspiration, Siobhan was the boss of the VGA. Although in her forties at the time, Siobhan had suffered a major accident in her twenties that completely wiped out her memory. In the absence of evidence to the contrary, she behaved (and still does) like someone twenty years younger. I was blown away. Siobhan has a unique gift for combining absolute professionalism with precision thought and astounding kindness. If she hadn't been married (I clocked the ring), I'd have gone down on one knee there and then.

We got on like a house on fire. Siobhan had drawn up a list of potential professions and asked me my opinion of it. I couldn't resist it: 'You're charging me two hundred pounds, and you've got no bloody idea?' I teased. Her guffaw told me we'd be firm friends. That night, I wrote her a letter. The contents have long disappeared from my memory but I do recall the high gag content. The call came through two days later. 'You're a writer,' she declared. 'Start writing.'

I waited a month. It was June 1986 and I had a long-standing date with football's World Cup. Once Maradona had lifted the trophy for Argentina, I bought a word processor and did as I was told. For a month, I wrote garbage, PURE drivel – I could *feel* the cobwebs in my brain, but at least I had somewhere to start. I'd written about rock music for a newspaper while a student at 'the Poly' and went back to what I knew.

And then it clicked: precisely thirty days after I'd restarted writing, I composed a set of reviews I knew would get noticed. By the beginning of September, I had my own column in a magazine called *Bang*. Six months later, I was a rock critic for the *Mail on Sunday*, the *London Daily News* (Robert Maxwell's ill-fated rival to London's *Evening Standard*) and *Company* magazine. Within a year, I had more work than I could handle.

I should have been thrilled – and I was, for about six months. Deep down, I was troubled, miserable, at times suicidal. I was a member of pop's inner circle, I was hanging out with the in-crowd, but the deep-rooted wretchedness just wouldn't shift. To the neutral observer, I had it all: a stunning blonde girlfriend who came to stay at weekends, a sports car (Lotus Esprit, thank you very much) and a job that allowed me to indulge my obsession – but it wasn't enough. I fell victim to sleep disorders and stress-related illnesses and felt an ever-greater reluctance to leave the house. I was imploding.

And now it would end. I'm about to be free. The lift is still falling. Just seconds to go.

It's the moment of impact. The lights explode. The door caves in as metal crumples towards me, the lift indicator is torn from its sockets. The sound is so deafening it must have been heard on the other side of Manhattan.

But something is wrong. For a moment, I can't work out what it is. Then, with a start, comes realisation:

I am still alive.

The shock has a numbing effect. Then terror appears. The lift is still moving beneath me. This tin coffin has crashed between floors and is hanging by a thread.

I wasn't scared until now. The prospect of survival has caught me by surprise.

Debris surrounds me – shards of woods and metal parted from ceiling and walls. I think about shouting but hardly dare to breathe. The slightest vibration of sound might snap the thinnest of cords that connects me to existence.

Surely someone must have heard? But no one appears. I have to find a way out and the lift is still shuddering.

To my right, approximately four feet away, is a phone. I've no way of telling if it's still connected. As the lift sways from side to side, I start to inch forward.

The first step is horrific. I put my weight down as softly as I can but feel the mechanism shift. Three big steps or six short ones? I go for the latter, figuring less weight improves the odds. No one will ever believe this, if I survive.

I reach the phone and gingerly pick up the receiver.

'Can I help you?' asks a voice.

'I'm in one of your lifts,' I reply. Suddenly, I come over all British. 'I'm afraid it has crashed.'

The answer is astonishing.

'No it hasn't.'

Now I lose it.

'It bloody well has,' I scream. 'Get me out now.'

The penny has dropped. 'I'll get on to maintenance,' the operator gulps.

I try to stay calm. Not easy when you're swaying in the darkness in a lift suspended several hundred feet in mid-air.

I wait three, four, five minutes. Almost ten have passed before voices echo in the lift shaft above.

'Are you OK?'

'Just about,' I reply, trying to sound urgent but calm. 'What the hell happened?'

'You crashed between the eighth and ninth floors. We're going to try and move the lift half a floor down.'

This is too much.

'Don't you xxxxing dare!' I rage. 'This lift is on a knife edge. The slightest movement could sent it straight down.'

Above me, I hear heads being scratched.

'OK,' he sighs. 'We'll work something out.'

How very reassuring.

All went quiet for another few minutes. I imagined ambulances being summoned, NYPD screaming through the streets of Central Park West and an expectant crowd gathering in the lobby below, craning their necks up at the unfolding drama – none of which, as it turned out, was happening.

I heard the sound of crunching metal above me. Then voices and a shaft of light. Lift doors were being jemmied open on the ninth floor.

I looked up in nervous anticipation and saw a face. 'Give me your hands,' came the instruction.

I was far from keen. The lift was still on a hair trigger. If the displacement caused by shifting weight caused it to drop, I would be sliced in half.

I reached up and grabbed two forearms wreathed in muscle. I felt my feet leave the floor, my torso hit the corridor carpet and I rolled my legs clear of the gaping elevator.

I was going to live.

The maintenance pair looked as shocked as I was. They had no idea why the lift hadn't plunged all the way to the bottom. My survival was a freak.

I was shaking, my legs were unsteady, I could barely talk. They asked if I wanted to take the remaining elevator to the lobby. My look suggested the idea was completely insane.

When we reached the mezzanine, my friend Joel was waiting to greet me. 'I've just been in a lift crash,' I sighed. He laughed. Then he saw my expression and noticed the 'Out of order' sign on the elevator. Joel went a pale shade of puce.

In the best tradition of Buck Rogers, I was determined to get straight back on the horse. Joel and I marched round to the Empire State Building and took a lift to the top. I almost passed out.

With hindsight, it's clear that I was in a deep state of shock. I even paid my bill at the hotel. Many people would have been struck by their outrageous good fortune and vowed to devote their lives to the sick and the poor.

Not me. I had to start with myself. I was a mess.

Returning to London, I noticed a rising sense of panic in familiar situations. I had to keep getting off London's Underground trains. Journeys that should have taken forty minutes seemed to be lasting several hours. On more than one occasion, nowhere near my destination, I had to get out and walk. The malaise soon spread to aeroplanes. On a short flight to Scotland for a journalistic assignment, my discomfort was so acute that I managed to spread it to several other passengers. I had a rampant case of Post-Traumatic Stress Disorder.

I was referred to Dr Thomas Farewell, one of the most eminent psychotherapists in the UK and a wise old owl. He, in turn, sent me to a hypnotherapist who opened up a whole new can of worms. I refused to co-operate.

To the chagrin of the hypnotherapist, I insisted on sitting bolt upright and remaining entirely lucid throughout the session. He wasn't going to get anything from me. But he did. Regressing back into childhood, I recovered memories of long-buried sexual abuse inflicted by strangers on a skiing trip when I was five. The memories had always been there but the sheer terror of the incident had kept them at bay. Even now, I wasn't ready to work through what had happened; that someone else knew was enough. This was the root of my deep-seated dis-ease. This was why I had been surrendered to death in the lift. I would be free! This revelation set me off in a whole new course of personal exploration. It's a journey that will take me the rest of my life. It's a journey that has led me to writing this book. I began with the Inner Game.

The founder of modern coaching is Tim Gallwey, a new-age, Californian ex-tennis-pro. Gallwey noticed, while he played, a voice in his head that would bark out a series of instructions – 'Extend your right arm!', 'Hit it hard!', 'Don't lose concentration!'. Gallwey's genius was to invent a method of distracting the voice, thus enabling latent talent to shine through. In its simplest terms, Gallwey's method helped tennis players 'get out of their own way'.

I started to apply Inner Game principles to the rest of my life. Within a month, I was appointed TV critic of the *Sun*. Professional and social opportunities kept falling into my lap. I'd even find parking spaces in rush hour.

Siobhan had alerted me to the revolutionary new science of NLP – Neuro-Linguistic Programming. One of the many virtues of NLP is that it enables those who have endured life-changing traumas to stop their past from running their present. Siobhan strongly advised me to enrol on an NLP course. In February 1996, I finally did.

The prospect was hideous – twenty days spread over five months, each interminable module stretching from Thursday to Sunday. I'd also heard rumours about the kind of people who attended such courses: losers, rejects and oddballs, one and all (except me, *naturellement*). For the first five-and-a-half days, I was bored stiff.

While everyone around me took copious notes and beamed the beam of the converted, I shuffled in my seat and scoffed at their gullibility. Most of the time I spent staring out the window or wishing I was out playing golf. Each afternoon, I had a nap.

One of the most vocal individuals on the course was Paul Hornsey-Pennell. A cellist-child-prodigy turned author of a best-selling book about aloe vera, whatever problem was being discussed, Paul seemed to have it. I thought he was irritating. He thought my cynicism was an excuse for non-involvement. We took to each other immediately.

On the Friday afternoon of Module 2, I was having a nap on the floor – which, as it happens, was fine. The facilitator (how I hate that word), NLP guru Ian McDermott, had told us to come and go when we wanted; that our subconscious would tell us when to tune in. To my immense irritation, he was right. I woke up with a start to find the entire room buzzing with energy. Ian was talking about 'association' and 'dissociation', about choosing whether to be 'in' your body or watching from outside.

'Associated' people are inside their bodies looking out, keenly aware of feeling and sensation. 'Dissociated' individuals *think* instead of *be*, watching themselves from a distance rather than taking part in their lives. This was me. Abuse had kept me 'dissociated' for most of my life. Whatever I achieved, I felt nothing. Even sex was a numbing experience. Now, NLP had my attention. I knew why Siobhan had guided me here.

In order to illustrate each new technique, Ian would

invite one of the group to work through an unresolved 'issue'. In my usual spirit of participation, I'd vowed nothing on earth would persuade me to get up on stage. Now, I couldn't sprint up there fast enough.

'New Light Through Old Windows' was a technique designed to promote fresh learning from negative experiences. My childhood torment was classic material. In front of 85 strangers, I learned that I was no longer afraid, that I could cope with whatever challenges life provided. I learned that it was over, I learned to forgive, I learned I was *ready*. I walked out that night feeling physically lighter. For the first time in living memory, I was unreservedly joyous. I drove home listening to Radiohead's CD *The Bends*, singing along with a lack of restraint that alarmed several small children.

I quickly learned something else. It was obvious that I had a gift for coaching. Ian would split the group into pairs and give us an hour to work through solutions. Everyone I worked with experienced rapid results; my 'client' would be sorted in 10–15 minutes. People were queuing up to take me to lunch in order to sort out their problems.

From then on I just sucked up everything I was taught. I was first in the room for the next three modules, absorbing every iota of knowledge that I could from this extraordinary learning. I discovered how to change state in a moment, how to be buzzing at work and sleepy in bed (instead of the other way round). I found out how to communicate effectively with anyone on the planet – NLP has identified that human beings are either visual, auditory or kinaesthetic and each group has its own 'language'. I learned how to wipe out phobias and even slow down time.

My friends began to notice a change. Tentatively, at first, they even asked me to help with an assortment of issues. Hearing them glowing with delight at what they experienced provided deep pause for thought. I started applying the learning to golf – both to my own game, which was passable though far from outstanding, and to helping those I played with. My first 'client' won the first event we prepared for. He won the next one too. Then I won two trophies of my own, but I knew I was only scratching the surface. I learned about life coaching, executive coaching and Gestalt. I enrolled on courses about family issues, relationship dynamics and, of course, sports psychology.

And so it went on. I was gathering learning purely for its own sake with no intention of forging a new career. My clients (rapidly growing in number) were experiencing significant breakthroughs and it wasn't costing them a penny. All the while, I was swapping notes with Paul Hornsey-Pennell. He, too, had been through a mountain of courses and was applying the learning with life-changing results. We decided to combine our knowledge and experience. In 2001, Paul and I began working with golfers and even charged one or two.

Paul and I were exploring a number of golf-related options when I sat down one evening to watch a football match between Birmingham and Aston Villa. It was hardly a contest. Birmingham were already two goals to the good when an incident occurred that made headlines all over the globe. Villa's centre-half, Olof Mellberg, took a throw-in which rolled gently and harmlessly towards their own goalkeeper, Peter Enckelmann. To the amazement of everyone present, and all those who witnessed the moment on TV, Enckelmann allowed a ball that was hardly moving to roll under his foot and into an unguarded net. Time seemed to stand still. Enckelmann was too stunned to move, his features frozen in a pallor of shock. To add to the agony, a jeering Birmingham fan leapt out of the crowd and stood in front of the goalkeeper, taunting Enckelmann for his error.

Next morning, I was on talkSPORT Radio's *Breakfast Show* to discuss the incident. Word had got round of my work with golfers and I'd become something of a pundit on sports matters. Aston Villa had a big game against Everton coming up at the weekend and the presenter asked me if their manager, ex-England boss Graham Taylor, should drop Peter Enckelmann. I did not feel that hiding the goalkeeper away was a practical solution, and described some of the techniques that a sports psychologist would employ to restore Enckelmann's confidence.

Once the radio broadcast had ended, I got in the car and drove to a meeting. Halfway towards my destination, I decided it was time to stop playing the pundit and put theory into practice. I put a call through to Paul: 'Please get on the phone to Villa and see if you can get through to Graham Taylor.' Paul is a man of astonishing persistence. He rang on the hour, every hour. All day. Graham's secretary patiently recorded each call and did so the following day when Paul rang again . . . and again.

Graham Taylor is anything but the hapless 'turnip' slaughtered by the press during his spell as England manager. He is phenomenally bright, impeccably courteous and a fabulous raconteur. It was typical of Graham that he should have called Paul back that evening to tell us that Peter was fine and Aston Villa would not be needing our help. It was equally typical that he should ring back the following day to say Peter was not all right after all and could we be at the training ground at 10 a.m. the next morning?

This was just my sort of job. We were about to work with a goalkeeper who had committed one of the biggest howlers in the history of the Premiership barely three days earlier. In forty-eight hours, the same goalkeeper would go out and play in front of forty thousand people who would remind him of that mistake every time he touched the ball. Bring it on!

Graham pulled Peter Enckelmann out of training and gave us as long as we needed. For half an hour, we talked about anything but football. Peter was far from the stereotypical sportsman: he was bright, thoughtful and sensitive. We talked about his Finnish homeland, mathematics and cricket. Then we got down to work. By midday, I was more than confident that our man would be fine. We had removed all trace of trauma and reinstalled a sense of personal conviction and clarity.

Come Sunday, Aston Villa won 3–2 and Peter Enckelmann was Man of the Match. I was relieved but not, in truth, all that surprised. My clients won, they always did. That may sound boastful but, thirty years ago, scientists believed human beings utilised only 20% of their brainpower. (That figure is actually much closer to 1%.) What I do – and did then – is help people access their unrealised psychological potential. They do and they win. The opposition do not and they lose.

Word was out. We were asked to work with several other Premiership sides. Golfers, cyclists, rugby internationals and distance runners seemed to materialise from all angles. Paul and I were tearing round the country working with two or three clients in a day, helping them prepare for sporting events that would be seen by millions.

When the season ended, Paul and I parted company and I teamed up with another highly respected sports psychologist, Martin Perry. Together, we began to create what would eventually become 'Evolutionary Golf', a series of techniques that go to the heart of my work and translate across all areas of life.

Non-golfers – bear with me. The reason the game is so addictive is that golf holds up a mirror to an individual's personality. Golfers who rush round the golf course rush through their lives. Golfers who breathe fire on the course are usually raging infernos in the rest of their lives.

The basis of Evolutionary Golf is *connection*. Most golfers approach each round in one of several states:

Expectation
Panic

Optimism
Despair
Recklessness
Fear of failure
Calmness
Agitation

Evolutionary Golf puts golfers absolutely *in the moment*. By maximising 'body sense' and putting the mind in neutral, anxiety vanishes and skill levels soar. Evolutionary Golf uses breathing, energy and colour to create a new kind of game altogether.

A quick example. At one of our first meetings, I was standing over the ball with a five iron in my hand when Martin asked me to hit a 'white' shot. I had no idea what he was talking about but a white parabola arcing high into the sky entered my mind. To my utter disbelief, the ball traced the very same arc and landed ten feet from the hole. 'Now,' he said, 'hit a red shot.' This time the flight was much lower, a piercing trajectory that never rose more than fifteen feet off the grass. Once again, the ball followed the same flight as I'd envisioned, pitched forward and rolled up onto the green. We experimented with blue shots, orange and yellow.

I discovered something profound that day, something that you will discover for yourself as you progress through this book. Mystical as this may sound, connection is one of the great secrets shared by high achievers. They maintain a sense of communion with their work, with their passion and with their purpose, drawing inspiration from everything that crosses their path.

All you have to do is connect . . .

Thousands of businesses stage golf days each year all over the UK. For the most part, these events are absolutely identical. Most of their clients can't even be invited – they've never played golf or don't have a handicap. To get round that problem, Martin Perry and I developed an event we call 'Golf for Non-Golfers'. In half an hour, anyone who has only occasionally (or never) picked up a club will find themselves hitting the ball 150–200 yards. It's a great day out and a spectacular demonstration of what human beings can do when they *stop trying* and connect with who they really are.

At one of these days, I was working with Karen, the Managing Director of an executive recruitment consultancy. We were on the putting green and she couldn't get the ball near the hole.

'How would it be,' I suggested 'if you stopped trying?' I might as well have been speaking Swahili.

'I always try,' she insisted. 'It's just what I do.'

'What do you do if trying doesn't work?' I inquired.

'I just try harder,' Karen declared, shoving another putt two foot wide of the hole. I removed the club from Karen's hand.

'What might happen,' I suggested, 'if you replaced trying with having fun? Instead of thinking about holing a putt, make your goal to have as much fun as possible on each shot.'

A look of confusion crossed Karen's face but she decided that humouring the coach would be the best policy.

'No trying,' I reiterated, handing back the club. 'Simply have as much fun as you can.'

Karen relaxed in front of my eyes. Her breathing deepened, the frown on her forehead disappeared and so did the next three putts – into the middle of the hole. Karen became visibly emotional. She asked to excuse herself for a few moments and walked away to the side of the green. Upon her return, she came straight to the point.

'That was incredible,' she said, 'but also disturbing. When I set up my company, the main objective was to have fun. Instead, I got bogged down in running the business, making a profit and taking care of customers. To be honest, I've been thinking of packing it in. The company is getting me down, I don't know why I do it any more. That exercise caught me totally off guard. I'd completely forgotten that having fun could be so effective. I feel angry that I've wasted so much time "trying". From tomorrow morning, everything we do will have some element of fun.'

Anything is possible

In the summer of 2003, I was on a train to somewhere exotic (Bolton, actually) when my phone rang. Ten minutes later, I'd been invited to appear in one of the most ambitious series that the BBC had ever mounted.

The Challenge was extraordinary in scope and ambition. The BBC had drawn up a list of the eight toughest sports events in the world and was planning to enter amateurs in each. No one would be allowed to take part in a sport (including ultra marathons, endurance skiing, mountain climbing) in which they'd had any previous experience.

To their credit, the production team realised that survival (let alone success) demanded arming the participants with an array of psychological tools that they could call upon in moments of stress (i.e. most of the time). There was one big catch (it would turn out to be the first of many). Preparing participants for the kind of gruelling events that constitute Adventure Racing normally takes 2–3 years. I would have 1–2 months and no more than three sessions with each contestant.

Physical fitness on *The Challenge* was entrusted to Greg Whyte of the British Olympic Association. As heat exhaustion, altitude sickness and sleep deprivation were not issues I had often faced when working with Premiership footballers, I asked Greg to put me in touch with the BOA's Head of Sports Psychology, Andy Lang. When I spoke to Andy, he just laughed. 'There ARE no psychological tools for dealing with these issues,' he chuckled. I was going to have to create them – and I did. Many of those brand-new tools were shown during the series; others I'll be covering in this book.

Filming *The Challenge* was a pulsating, exhausting, unparalleled adventure. It stretched everyone involved – contestants, crew, production team – beyond that which they had previously believed to be their physical, emotional and psychological limits – me included. Lives were arguably dependent on what I did. In order to enable participants to cope with the sheer brutality of their challenges and return in one piece, I had to find new levels of resource and creativity. The results speak for themselves. Two of the contestants won their races against world-class opposition. A third won his individual category and set a new World Record.

What they discovered – and what you are about to discover – is that achievement begins where the comfort zone ends. **Life begins when you DARE.**

The Challenge was the culmination of ten years' work. By the time the series finished airing in Spring 2005, I'd developed an entirely new raft of techniques. I couldn't help wishing that I could go back in time and share many of them with the contestants. You and I won't have that problem.

The Challenge demonstrated, beyond all reasonable doubt, what human beings are capable of achieving when they know what they want. ***When they really, absolutely, without the slightest scintilla of doubt, know what they want.*** More is needed, of course. Clarity of intent must be allied to absolute commitment, robust self-belief and resilience in the face of unforeseen setbacks. This book will give you all these and more.

One of the great things about working with high achievers in business and sport is that I get to observe, at close quarters, why they succeed. Do not be fooled. Fear of failure, fear of rejection, fear of humiliation are just as real at the top as at the bottom. The difference is that high achievers relish the opportunity to confront their demons and emerge stronger still.

Dare

'Courage is being scared to death but saddling up anyway.'

JOHN WAYNE

This book is a joint effort. Read it *only* if you feel an outstanding life is waiting to be lived. Read it *only* if you know you haven't touched what you could be. Read it *only* if you are ready to do something about it.

Do you know where you are going? Do you know what you want? Do you know how to get it? Let's go to work.

SESSION I

Behind the Mask

When you walk through the door of my office, it doesn't matter who you are. I work with international footballers from across the globe, world-class rugby stars and multitalented athletes, Olympians and golfers. I also work with professional people, executives, housewives, teenagers and children. I repeat: when you walk through the door of my office, it doesn't matter who you are.

What does matter to me is why you are here. What matters to you is how to get over whatever it is that happens to be in your way – fast! That is what I do. When you walk out of my office a couple of hours later, you will feel differently about yourself and your place in the world. You will feel optimistic, unbounded, uplifted. You will have reconnected with your sense of personal direction.

You will, instantly, stand apart from 99% of the population. Let's be clear about this: walk down any street, any time of day, and the vast majority of people you will see are lost or overwhelmed. Their lives have little meaning; their fundamental goal is to get to the end of their days in as little pain as possible. You have a choice. To be just like them or to DARE to be different. Which will it be?

Opening this book represents the start of a contract between us. Unlike most contracts, the terms are really quite simple:

a) I provide step-by-step guidelines that will lead you to the life you want.
b) You follow them.

This is not a manual for the lazy. However intently you study the text, this book will not help unless you do something with it. If you want a 'nice read', buy a novel.

I will set out your plan of action in *exactly* the same way as I would if you were sitting in front of me, but I can't make you do it. That's the part of our contract I trust you to fulfil. And, while you are enjoying the immediate benefits of putting our plan into action, I know that you will.

Please make sure you've got a notebook handy. *Pick a notebook that you like*, one you will want to have around. Your notebook is your treasure trove. As we continue, it will not only become a repository of priceless information about you but also be a map of the route from where you are now to where you want to be. Restrain the impulse to buy the first notebook you stumble across, especially if it's grey. *You are not grey.* Your life is not grey (or it won't be!). Buy a notebook that reflects how you want to feel. Let's get started.

Who are you? and what do you want?

'Who am I?' is the question that has haunted human

beings since the dawning of time. The question is pivotal to self-realisation. Unless you know who you are, how can you know what you want? How can you design a life to suit without a razor-sharp sense of whom it is meant for? Most people, frankly, are just guessing.

I once worked with a Chief Executive who discovered, during the course of our sessions, that his life's purpose was to be a songwriter. Fortunately, he had the money to pursue this new calling and so he quit his job and went to make a new life in Los Angeles. Not everyone is so fortunate. I have worked with TV presenters who wanted to be doctors, cameramen who longed to write copy for advertising agencies and golfers who wanted to be teachers. But they were stuck . . . stuck with mortgages, stuck with school fees, stuck with partners who would not take kindly to a sharp reversal in financial fortunes.

In order to understand fully what you want – and stop heading in totally the wrong direction – you need to know who you are. This isn't as hard as it sounds; all it takes is some honesty and commitment as you'll see. The rewards are great, the pitfalls enormous and getting it wrong is why most people are lost.

Just the job, or not . . .

Vocational misdirection is a modern epidemic. It affects, according to surveys, 99% of the workforce. All right, there's no survey, I invented that bit – but how many people would be doing what they are doing if they knew then what they know now?

It begins in childhood. 'What do you want to be when you grow up?' is, on the surface, an innocent-enough question. I consider it to be one of the most pernicious inquiries on the face of the planet. What age were you first asked the question – eight, ten, twelve, fourteen? How *on earth* were you meant to know? Did the answer you gave come from the heart, or was it designed to please the person asking the question?

I remember writing an essay in class when I was nine. The essay topic was 'What I Want To Be When I Grow Up'. At the time, my favourite TV programme was *The Man From UNCLE*. Each Thursday night from 8 to 9 p.m. on BBC1, Robert Vaughn and David McCallum would save the world from the evils of THRUSH (don't be silly, this was an organisation of criminal master-minds). I badly wanted to be David McCallum's character, Illya Kuryakin. Admittedly he was only the sidekick to Vaughn's Napoleon Solo, but he seemed to tell most of the jokes and didn't have to kiss any girls.

So it was that I called my essay 'I Want To Be A Spy'. Our teacher, whose own life goal was clearly to teach a class of nine-year-olds who thought she was a dragon, flew into a rage. My ambition was 'ridiculous'; I was a 'dreamer'. I was told to rewrite my essay and come up with something sensible. So I said I wanted to sell shoes. The 'tick' I received suggested this was much more appropriate for a child of my capabilities.

At secondary school, aged sixteen, just before our O-level exams, each member of the class was allocated fifteen whole minutes with a 'careers adviser'. Attendance wasn't even compulsory but it got me out of physics. Entering the room, I was met by a fug of smoke emanating from the pipe of a man in his fifties. He looked like a civil servant, was transparently bored and spoke in a monotone. He had never met me before and we would never meet again. He told me I should be a mathematician. I was clearly in the presence of a lunatic. It was touch and go whether I would even pass Maths O-level. I smiled politely and tried not to inhale.

I paid a high price for having no idea what to do with my life, though not as high as Leo, one of my lifelong friends. I used to travel into London on the Tube each morning with Leo. This was during the early eighties. Margaret Thatcher was Prime Minister, Duran Duran were top of the charts and I still had black hair. At the time, I was a barrister and Leo was an accountant. We both loathed what we did but there was one crucial difference. As a pupilled barrister, I was paid not a penny. I may have left the Bar on a matter of principle but lack of financial remuneration made it an easy decision.

Leo was already well paid. He could afford a car and smart clothes (not that he ever bought any) and was saving up for a flat. Money was a trap and Leo was ambushed. He became a partner in a smart West End practice and his name appeared proudly on the letterhead. But Leo hated accountancy. By nature, my friend is deeply artistic. Leo should have worked in a fashion house or a gallery or the music industry. Leo is a colourful, warm, sensitive soul who lost 'himself' in the dis-guise of an accountant. Inside, Leo was suffering. Medical science has not advanced sufficiently for doctors to make a definitive connection, but Leo contracted Parkinson's Disease at the tender age of 35. His body had rebelled against the lifestyle he'd chosen. By his early forties, Leo had no option but to retire from work altogether.

Shortly before he did so, Leo and I went for a drive. Without premeditation, I asked him a question:

'Imagine you were still working as an accountant in your sixties,' I posited. 'How does that make you feel?'

Leo went ashen. The look he gave me suggested the prospect was too terrible to contemplate; he'd projected an image of himself twenty years hence and saw nothing but utter despair.

Leo has now begun the painful process of mid-life redirection. He travels, he reads, he thinks. In time, he will find the path to redemption. But the twenty-year detour need never have happened if he had answered carefully, and truthfully, the question 'Who am I?'

True or False Self

What we are about to undertake may be the most important exercise in the entire book. Forget that, it *is* the most important exercise in the entire book. Without question, it is the source of the most profound changes that I see in my clients. Taking this exercise on board is the key that unlocks the door to their *truth*.

Every single one of us carries around two personae – our 'True Self' and our 'False Self'. Our True Self is our spirit, our nature, **our essence**. This is who we really are. Most people have buried this aspect of their nature so deeply they have forgotten it ever existed. Think of a time when you were truly 'you'. Pure you, undiluted you, authentic, unadulterated, absolute you. When was that? What were you doing?

For sportsmen, this is easy. They are in True Self at the zenith of their competitive powers – holing the winning putt on the final green, playing a passing shot down the line on match point or scoring the winner in front of fifty thousand adoring supporters. Most of my life-coaching clients have to dig deeper. With a little prompting, they remember when they truly felt *alive*. It may have been dancing without restraint to their favourite tune, building sandcastles on the beach as a child or cooking a special meal for their loved one.

The desperate truth is that few people experience their True Self for more than fleeting moments in adulthood. The True Self is too precious, too private, too vulnerable to display to the world. Hiding it away means your secret is safe. However, hide it away *too well* and you forget it exists.

Most people spend the vast majority of their lives in False Self. The False Self is a mask, a costume, a disguise. It is the image of ourselves that we want the world to see, it is what we think we need to do and become in order to make ourselves acceptable. The False Self is grey, lacklustre and dull. It is denial. It is demeaning. It is a *lie*. The seeds of the False Self are sown in childhood. Children absorb their parents' attitudes, beliefs and neuroses and adopt them as their own. This is what is called 'good behaviour'. Good behaviour is rewarded with approval, cuddles and presents. The instances when such behaviour is appropriate for these poor offspring will be incredibly (I would say freakishly) few – but the Parent Trap has been set.

Let me make a distinction between values and conformity. I am absolutely in favour of parents establishing value-based norms for their children. Honesty, decency, self-respect, integrity – all these are essential for productive coexistence and avoiding imprisonment. However, we have all either met or read about dictatorial elders passing down codes of their own invention on tablets of stone. Whether their motives lie in preserving tradition or enjoying the sight of others jumping with each crack of the parental whip – blind obedience wrecks lives. Children who reject the mores of their parents are frequently labelled rebellious, naughty or downright 'impossible'. The number of high achievers who fall into this bracket is out of proportion. This may not be a complete coincidence.

The False Self lies at the root of many of the ailments that currently ravage society. Given that the vast majority of people spend their entire lives pretending to be something that they manifestly are not, the plethora of illness and disenchantment is hardly surprising. Living in False Self explains why so many people are locked into the wrong job, marry the wrong partner and follow a religion they no longer (if ever they did) believe in. Wearing the mask for long enough has persuaded them that this is *who they are*.

Worst of all, the mask has a devastating impact upon self-confidence. I define self-confidence as *a relationship of trust between 'you' and 'you'* – the power of self-reliance when the going gets tough. Living in False Self removes that power. If you don't know who you are, how can you trust your own judgement? How can you make decisions that are appropriate for you?

Counteracting this phenomenon forms the epicentre of my life-coaching work. I help clients remove their masks, take off their costumes and reconnect with their True Self. Doing so provides a joyous sense of personal liberation. I get to watch people *reclaim themselves* – it is what makes what I do so rewarding. Now it is your turn – but first, a small word of warning.

Stepping into True Self will give you back your appetite for life, it will provide fresh impetus, motivation and hope. It will allow you to see that your dreams are anything but ridiculous, that what you want is entirely appropriate, that the life you desire was waiting to be claimed all along. Please notice I don't use the word 'grasp' but 'claim'. Your True Self is your birthright. You don't have to grab it or snatch it or (that word again) 'try'. It was simply biding its time until your return.

However, truth and falsehood cannot live side by side. The life your True Self will lead may be quite different to the path your False Self has followed. Your True Self will simply not tolerate the degree of compromise or dissatisfaction that you have lived with until now.

> The True Self is clear, it is untarnished, it is a laser beam that will burn away everything that does not chime with your inner truth.

Change is inevitable. I warn all my clients before beginning this process that they may have some tough decisions to make once they reconnect with themselves. Career goals may need to be rethought; relationships may require swift revaluation. Your True Self may not tolerate the environment in which you've been living or the food you have been eating. You may find yourself wearing different clothes, pursuing new interests, taking up a musical instrument or even (steady now) pursuing some exercise. You *will* do all those things and more.

Finding your True Self

I want you to recall a time when you were absolutely Your Self, when you were absolutely, unmistakably, uncompromisingly *you*. You felt passionate, supercharged, wonderful, completely and utterly in the moment. What were you doing?

Were you walking to school holding your mum's hand? Acting in a play? Receiving a prestigious award that you knew you deserved? Nailing the biggest deal of your career? Scoring a century? Holding the love of your life in your arms? I want you to recall *everything* about that experience. See it as if it was happening now:

Where did it take place?
At what time of day?
How old were you?
Who else was present?
Was it sunny or gloomy?

What were you wearing?
Were you moving or stationary or both?
How did you feel?
What did you say?
What was the response?

Some people can recall every detail of the experience but you may only get a ten-second 'film clip'. This makes no difference at all. Just *be there*. Enjoy those fantastic feelings all over again. Give the entire experience as much colour and sound and emotion – **especially emotion** – as you can. I want you to feel an overpowering sense of joy as each layer of memory is added. THIS is your True Self. Take time to reconnect. Take time to lock into its wavelength. Take time to feel the strength that it gives you.

You may start to feel empowered, rejuvenated, re-energised, perhaps even (don't worry, I'm not about to go all evangelical) *reborn*. But many people also feel aggrieved. They are saddened that they have been separated from this essence, from their source, from their truth for so long. You may feel confused, resentful or angry that you could ever have let this happen to Your Self. Take a deep breath. Go back a few pages if necessary and remind yourself how easy it is to absorb others' values, judgements and opinions as if they were your own. I wonder if you really had any choice?

OK, so you have pinpointed your memory. Now I want you to brainstorm. **I want you to write in your notebook a series of adjectives that describe you during that experience.** Among those that often come up are the following:

Accomplished	Inspiring
Articulate	Magnificent
Capable	Nourished
Charming	On course
Childlike	Overjoyed
Committed	Powerful
Confident	Productive
Decent	Resilient
Elated	Safe
Energetic	Secure
Graceful	Supported
Happy	Unstoppable
Impressive	Untainted

See if you can come up with a list of 8–12 words that encapsulated the 'you' in that movie and write them down.

Sit back, take a moment and look at that list objectively. Does that sound like the 'True' you? Run through the movie in your mind one more time and experience the emotions once again. Is there anything you've just realised that needs to be added? Read the list out aloud. It should feel solid, like a brick in a wall that's back where it belongs. Your list should 'slot' into your subconscious like an old friend coming home. You have just *reconnected*. Take it in, soak it up.

Do you recognise this person? Do you remember this person? Are you ready to *become* this person again? Are you sick and tired of being anything else? Are you ready to stop wearing the costume? Is the price of pretending too high?

Occasionally – very occasionally – a small shard of doubt remains. For most people, the prospect of reconnection is so overwhelming that living a lie for one more second is simply unacceptable, but one in a hundred holds back. Although desperate to shed a skin that never fit in the first place, they are afraid of the reaction from others. 'They might not like the real me,' is a perfectly understandable response. They understand the you they know. *That* you fits in their world. *That* you is familiar.

This must be dealt with. I ask these good souls, who have already suffered for far too long, what it will cost them to remain in False Self for the rest of their lives? Few even need to answer. The look on their faces speaks of hopelessness, depression, dependency, loss of expectation, even surrendering the will to live altogether. If you still remain hesitant, ask yourself the same question. The answers will leave no space for further delay.

I'll be honest, the second part of the process isn't much fun. However, it only takes a few moments and blows the False Self into a million pieces. **I want you to think of a time – and there will have been many – when you were in the dis-guise of False Self.** It might have been a particularly dull meeting at work, or pretending to enjoy the company of someone who bored you, or attending a party you longed to escape from. Maybe it was being with an ex-partner who never felt 'right' – but other people kept saying was perfect for you. In each case, something felt 'wrong'. This was not the person you set out to be.

Good. Now, just as before, stay with it. See yourself in that moment (it only has to be a moment, we don't need a movie this time). **What adjectives describe you in that place?** My clients usually spit out some of the following, their faces bearing a look of disgust:

Anxious	Miserable
Bored	Self-indulgent
Defocused	Sluggish
Demotivated	Snappy
Dissatisfied	Tired
Fat	Unconfident
Frustrated	Unsettled
Immobile	Weak
Indolent	

Now make a list of your own and write it in your notebook. Don't stop until you can hardly bear to think about what you're writing.

Look at your list. How does it feel? Pretty unpleasant, I would guess. This is certainly not someone you are proud of or would even much care to be around. This is your False Self. Do you want to be that person any more?

TIME FOR THE EXPLOSION

I want you to write out your two lists in bold letters. Your 'True Self' should be in your favourite colour – blue, red, lilac, cyan, whatever it is. If you are typing the list into a PC, do so in 24, 36 or 48 point.

I want the letters to be HUGE! You should be able

to see the ingredients of your True Self from across the other side of the room.

Now for the False Self. Once again, write or type out your list but *in much smaller script*. Forget the colours, we want this one to be as bland as possible. Stick it up on a wall beside your True Self list as a constant reminder of the contrast.

So now you know. Your True Self and False Self bear no resemblance to each other. One is rich in energy, life and possibility; the other is dispiriting, hopeless and dark.

BRINGING IT *ALIVE*

So far, so good, but the biggest step has yet to be taken. Bringing the distinction between True and False Self into consciousness is a deeply significant piece of work. Take time out if you need to dwell longer upon the information you have gleaned. However, what really matters is making it *live*. The challenge is not just knowing the difference between True and False Self but living in Truth every moment of each day.

There comes a time in any relationship between life coach and client when the need to go 'off piste' arises. This is one of those times. Some people may react with surprise to the process I am about to suggest. Ignore any such reaction. This is your False Self living in fear, telling you it is 'strange' or 'outrageous' or 'not the sort of thing I feel comfortable doing at all'. Do not be alarmed. No nudity is involved, you won't have to write to your MP.

Look at the list of adjectives that describe your True

Self. Return, for a few seconds, to the movie from which those characteristics were drawn. Enjoy the experience once again. Now – here's the off-piste bit – during that movie, *what kind of animal did you most resemble*? I told you it was outrageous. Most of my clients instinctively know which is 'their' animal. I have had lions, tigers, panthers, elephants, birds, monkeys, dogs, cats, dolphins, deer, penguins and polecats. My favourite, so far, was a peacock because it so clearly matched the client's extroverted personality. He was the sort of man who should have been born wearing a feather boa.

Which is your animal? Resist the temptation to be too analytical. What kind of creature leaps to mind and 'feels' right to you? Don't be defensive. No one else need ever know. You will notice a sense of connection when you've made the right choice. A sense of satisfaction, of pleasure – you just 'know'.

I want to return briefly to the False Self you've described. Have another look at the list. What species of animal does this bring to mind? I've had fat dogs, slugs, sloths, rats, mice, buzzards, lizards, worms, beetles, maggots, grubs and even a termite.

Now contrast your two creatures. Which of the two would you rather be? What would a lion/panther/ elephant do to a mouse/maggot/worm? Eat it! Squash it! DESTROY it! Which kind of creature are you going to be?

Understanding your True Self

This is a fabulous exercise to do in a group. It's one I use with corporate clients, although you can also have a lot of fun with friends lubricated by a few drinks.

Confident people get what they want in situations of conflict. The object of this exercise is to allow members of a team to reflect on their own particular styles and learn to adapt.

I write the names of 15–20 animals on sheets of paper and paste them around a room – giraffe, hyena, donkey, snake, lion, skunk, tortoise, monkey, mouse, chameleon, vulture, ostrich etc. I ask the audience if they ever felt they worked (or lived) in a jungle. Do colleagues or friends who seem to be decent, fair-minded people turn into sharks when you're not looking? Everyone is given a few minutes to walk round the room before standing under the poster of the animal they feel best represents them. If no animal quite fits the bill, you can write your own creature on spare sheets of paper.

This is a great way of gaining new insight into people you work or live with. Questions that provide talking points for hours include:

1. How do I resemble my animal? What are the good and bad points that we share?
2. Any surprises? Which of the animals chosen by other people do you feel are wrong? What would you have chosen for them?
3. Is there anyone in the room you find it hard to get along with? What would happen in a fight between your two creatures?
4. From what you've learned, how might changing your 'animal instincts' lead to better relationships?

Anyway, why is it so important to know the identity of your animal? What has this got to do with living in True Self?

I have met and worked with several practitioners in the field of kinesiology. One of them was a feisty, extremely abrupt, no-nonsense character who terrified the life out of most of her clients. In a former life, she was probably a matron at a boarding school.

However, her opinions were always good value, and one of her many interesting observations was that those of us living in Western civilisation spend far too much time in our heads. She was right. How much time do you spend each day 'thinking'? I don't mean thinking about things that matter, but all that random, jumbled-up, meaningless gobbledegook that rattles around your brain when *you're not even aware that it's happening*.

Let's take *today*, for example. How many discussions or arguments have you had with people *who weren't even there*? How much time have you wasted speculating about things that 'may be fantastic' or 'could be difficult' or 'might (or might not) work out'? How much time have you spent thinking about events which you have no way of controlling? You are not alone. This is most people, most of the time. All that energy, all that magnificent processing power is being wasted on complete and utter *garbage*!

Western society has lost the ability to dwell in the physical – in the body. It has forgotten how just to 'be', how to rest quietly, contentedly and peacefully without our overactive brains constantly grinding through the gears. *We are Human Beings not Human*

Doings. Yet, each day is a list of activities that must be completed. Why? So we can make another list for tomorrow, of course. When you are watching TV in the evening, what percentage of your attention is focused on whatever it is you are meant to be watching? And how much is taken up by distracting thoughts of what you haven't done or mustn't forget and had better write down?

Many clients come to me suffering from insomnia. The very first piece of advice I give them is to go home and remove the notebook from their bedside table. 'How did you know I have one?' is the astounded response. 'I'm a genius,' I reply.

> Nothing, but nothing, is less conducive to a good night's sleep than issuing an open invitation to your subconscious to wake you up – whenever it feels like it – with 'good ideas'.

After a few moments' thought, clients invariably admit that most of what they write down in the middle of the night turns out to be nonsense (not to mention, indecipherable nonsense). Be honest. How many truly great ideas have you had in the middle of the night? However, even bad ideas show that when we are sleeping – we are doing.

There is a choice. Human beings are complex and multifaceted creatures; but we are also spiritual, vegetable (no, this is not about sitting in front of the sport with beer and a burger – I'm talking about earthly connection) and physical. We need to get back in touch with our own bodies.

Living your True Self

Most people hate their bodies. They can't stand their own noses or stomachs or legs or feet or backsides. We are too fat, too thin, too tall, too short, too ugly, too pretty, too – you name it, we hate it. Body Fascism is rampant. We are continually judging ourselves and each other as if such evaluations serve any purpose. It all adds up to yet more pointless mental activity.

The next step towards True Self is about merging with your animal. This exercise is *only* to be carried out when you know you will not be disturbed. It demands absolute privacy but takes no more than five minutes the first time you do it and two or three minutes thereafter.

1. BREATHING
Find a comfortable chair and take three deep breaths in through the nose. Breathe in to the count of four, feeling the air moving down into the chest as it expands and enlarges. Hold the breath for a moment before releasing it out through your mouth, also to the count of four. Feel the air moving softly back into the atmosphere. Pause, and repeat the breathing twice more.

2. ANIMAL POSITIONING
Now, take up what I call the 'Animal Position':

- Cross your right ankle over your left ankle.
- Cross your right wrist over the left wrist, entwining your fingers underneath and turning upwards under the chin.
- Close your eyes.

3. VISUALISING

I want you to 'see' your animal in your mind. Not any member of the species you've chosen but *your* particular, special, unique animal. How big is it? How old is it? What kind of markings or colourings does it have? Are there any unusual or distinguishing features that will allow you to distinguish it immediately from other members of the herd, flock or pack? Look it in the eye. Know what it's thinking. Know how it feels. Know what it *wants*.

The next series of questions are really important:

Is it stationary?
Is it moving?
Is it *in a cage*? If so, let it out. *Open the cage.*

Most new animals move slowly at first. They have been penned in for so long that freedom of movement is beyond their comprehension. Be patient. Let your animal walk around – let it roam and let it stretch. Let it discover, let it explore, let your animal realise *it is free*. In time, it will learn to run or to fly or to charge. It will hunt, it will kill, it will *rule* its own world. Your animal will go back to doing whatever comes naturally. It will, once again, *be itself*.

The first time you do this exercise will bring a surge of recognition. *'This is "me".'* By the third or fourth time, you should know your animal inside out. You should have an intimate understanding of its features, movements, habits and qualities.

4. MERGING

Now, *I want you to merge*. Instead of watching from a distance, *get inside the skin of your animal*. Feel its power, its beauty, its *being*. Move with it, live inside it, *be* your animal. Observe the clarity, the ease, the absolute mastery of the world it inhabits and commands. Merging with your animal adds a physical depth to your True Self. It supplements the psychological process of seeing your list of adjectives in black and white with a physical sense of belonging inside your own skin.

Change will start to happen almost immediately. You will notice decisions are becoming easier, judgements are clearer; you will feel sharper and more energised. Irritations matter less: you are positive, determined, in tune, *clinical*. Others will notice a new sense of pride, a subtle but palpable boldness and, I warned you, a growing refusal to put up with old nonsense.

At the risk of sounding like a doctor prescribing a course of treatment, please, *please, please* repeat this exercise twice a day for at least a fortnight. The more you do it, the more resilient you will become, the stronger you will stand and the harder it will become to knock you off course. It only takes a couple of minutes, but your sense of personal power and potential will expand out of all recognition. Long-standing clients use this exercise all the time. They use it before a big meeting, when preparing to face world-class opponents or prior to spending a weekend with their in-laws. They disappear into bathrooms or side rooms or take a moment to themselves. They use it to gather their resources, to collect their thoughts and *to be*.

There is one short, final part to the exercise. You don't have to complete this but I strongly suggest that you do. It is a hugely effective method of crossing 'the bridge' and emerging back from your inner world into the one we inhabit.

Just before opening your eyes, put the fingers of your hands together to form a shape like a steeple. Breathing slowly, hold that position for 20–30 seconds. When you feel ready, let your eyes open.

So now you know. You have met your True Self. This is who you are. And it is PERFECT. But then, it always was.

The next challenge is to stand firm as the weeks, months and years go by. In the past, you have surrendered your identity, bit by bit, under the weight of external influences. Without knowing how it happened, you gave in to the pressures imposed by friends, family or colleagues. That will not, *must not* happen again. Standing in True Self just feels too fantastic to surrender at any price. The cost of living in False Self is far too high and you have paid it for quite long enough. You must become your own strongest ally, reinforcing the bond of trust between 'you' and 'you' that I have already described.

Reclaiming your True Self is not a cure for all known ills. You are still you, life will continue to present challenges and difficulties. What is different is the way you will respond from now on. Start to develop a muscle you may recognise. It is probably withered through lack of usage but reacts well to regular exercise. It's a muscle called CHOICE. Every time you are faced with a decision, ask yourself a question: *Is this really me?*

Does the Real Me – my True Self – want to be with that person, take that job, buy that shirt, go to that party, make that speech, stand in that queue (I don't do queues) or take that crap for one moment longer? Every time you are in any doubt, *stand in True Self*. You will soon notice the emergence of certainty. Keep exercising the muscle and people will think twice before crossing you.

Session Summary

This is THE pivotal chapter of the book. Do not move on until you have completed all the exercises. Do not move on until you:

i) have a clear and complete list of True Self qualities
ii) have a clear and complete list of False Self adjectives
iii) have a typed or written-out version of both lists which you have hung on a wall that you pass every day

 iv) have identified your True Self animal
  v) know the identify of your False Self creature
 vi) have been through the Animal exercise at least
   six times
 vii) are committed to staying in True Self no matter
   what.

Do not be tempted to skip any of these steps. Clients who do so find their coach smiling politely and telling them to come back when they have. *One look – and I know*. Those of us who live in True Self instantly recognise those who do not.

The Power of Want

Our first session has cleared a massive space in your psyche. In place of the fog from which you were trying to build a meaningful life, you now have the luxury of total visibility. You are standing in power – your power – and it is boundless. You must use it. This power creates an opportunity to structure a life that finally makes sense. Working up from foundations that are, at long last, secure, you can create the existence that was always meant to be yours. This is what we will begin to do in this chapter.

It is astonishing what is revealed in True Self. It's like putting on a new pair of glasses. You suddenly realise how out of focus your view of the world had become. Seeing everything the way it should be – the way it really is – provides a fresh outlook. You wonder why you put up with being short-sighted for so long.

Living in True Self has precisely that same impact. Life becomes better, sharper, clearer, easier. You no longer need to tiptoe around in a state of low-level anxiety. But this perspective has to be *used*.

The want contradiction

The Western world is built on ambition. Children are encouraged to strive, to forage, to work. 'No one,' they are told 'is going to hand it to you on a plate.' At the same time we are warned against wanting too much: our desires may turn out to be beyond us, or they might be too much to hope for (which won't stop us getting 'upset' if we don't get them).

On the one hand, want is 'a good thing' in that it is the fuel that powers the engine of purpose. On the other hand, if the price of not getting what we want is heartache, is it safe to want anything at all? It's time to make up your mind. Shall you want what you want or not?

Michael Douglas's Oscar-winning performance in *Wall Street* (1987) as Gordon Gekko (he of the 'Greed Is Good' philosophy) placed filmgoers in a quandary: whether to acknowledge that they secretly shared (in small or large part) Gekko's avaricious tendencies or whether to boo at the pantomime villain on screen.

Want is invariably cast as the bad guy. To want is 'selfish', 'egotistical' and 'bad form'. Much safer to set your sights low and play the hand you've been dealt. High achievers could not agree less. Seeking gratification by fair means or foul is clearly unacceptable; but wanting is not, and never was, the problem.

Flash back to childhood – what did you want? A doll? A ball? A swing? A party? A game? A hug? *Why did you want them?* Like most things about childhood, it's simple.

a) Because they made you happy.
b) Because it was just who you were.

There are two kinds of wants. The first include all those that meet a) and b) above. Yes, you want them because they'll make you happy – but so do most of the things we crave. What sets these 'innocent', authentic wants apart is that *they come from True Self*. These wants are easily recognised – they lead to fulfilment, self-expression and peace of mind. The more you get, the more of your True Self you become.

The second category is less appealing. This kind of want is the outcome of envy, greed, pride, one-upmanship, revenge or misanthropy. These wants are the product of *ego*. They are a way of saying 'I've got and you haven't'. They are adversarial, self-serving and distancing. It is these wants that have led people to question the virtue of ambition and have called into doubt the very reason for wanting.

Authentic wants are good for you

It is a fundamental characteristic of the human condition that we hate to be judged – even by ourselves. Most judgements centre around whether you are better or worse than anyone else – but you are not in a competition. There *is* no competition, not unless you choose to invent one.

Status envy occupies a large chunk of my coaching time; and by far the most common barometer that people use to assess 'How am I doing?' is money. As a way of shedding their obsession with judgement, I invite clients to use an indicator other than bank notes. Instead of money, I ask them to tell me: 'Who is the happiest person you know?' or 'Who is the wisest?' or 'Who is most alive?' And (for all these people) how important is money to *them*?

The silence that follows is often accompanied by a huge sigh of relief. Constantly comparing your job or bank account or marriage to those of friends or neighbours or members of your family is a massive, and totally unnecessary cause of stress. Just because everyone else is in a race doesn't mean you have to compete. Give yourself a break and get off the track. If you are in doubt about whether your wants are genuine, choose one and ask yourself, *Why do I want it?* Is your motivation rooted in Authenticity or in 'Me, Me, Me!'?

Authentic wants take you closer to your 'source' – to the part of you that is harmonious, happy, peaceful and supportive. Ego-based desires are about other people, not you – about showing or having or pretending. High achievers understand the distinction. While they may have set out to prove a point, they end up rediscovering themselves, and it's by being more of themselves that they move clear of the crowd.

The Big Questions about wanting

Three more BIG questions are coming up, next, for you to consider and answer:

1. What do you want to do?
2. Why do you want to do it?
3. How will your life be different (when you do)?

Think carefully before answering and make a note of whatever comes to mind. Resist the urge to censor yourself if what comes up doesn't seem to 'make sense'. Your answers will provide the foundation for everything that follows in the rest of the book.

QUESTION 1: WHAT DO YOU WANT TO DO . . . ?
. . . professionally, financially, personally and emotionally Stop right there. This is emphatically not about what you'd 'quite like' to do, or what would be 'nice', or what would be (heaven forbid!) 'all right, I suppose'. Much as I hate to borrow a phrase from the Spice Girls, a line from one of their songs hits the spot. I need to know what you 'really, really want' – to *achieve*. BIG distinction. This not about what you want to *happen* but what you want to *do*. This list is *active* – NOT passive. I want you to get into the habit of taking control, of ceasing to be 'resigned to your fate' or blown in the wind. Success is born of action. Action demands responsibility.

Dig DEEP. What are your cherished dreams – the ones that you tell no one about because you fear they would laugh? What ambitions did you have as a child or a teen that you 'had' to let go of because they seemed out of reach? What gives you a warm glow whenever the thought comes to mind? This does not have to be about winning the lottery, living in a mansion or scoring the winning goal in the World Cup Final. It might be about finding a new partner, living in the country or simply getting well. Still struggling? Let me make this even easier.

Study the following question and write down the first five answers that come into your head. Don't think, *write*.

What would I do if I wasn't afraid?
Puzzled by what you've just written? That's fine. These answers are never what you expect them to be. It's all the stuff you sort of knew but never managed to bring into consciousness.

Now give me five answers to this one:

What would I do if I knew I couldn't fail?
Some of the items on both lists will be the same. Inevitably, some of what you've written will raise more questions than answers but we'll deal with those later. Now (at last) you know what it is you are aiming to achieve; so, together, we will plot a route to bring it to fruition.

'Want power' in action Most of my work follows a similar pattern. Clients explain the nature of their problem and, over the course of a number of sessions, I devise an appropriate solution.

Making *The Challenge* for TV was different. I simply didn't have time for that kind of approach. In most cases, I only met my 'clients' two or three weeks before they had to climb Mount Everest, walk halfway across the North Pole or run six marathons across the Chilean desert in five days. I had to GIVE them what I knew they would need.

Fundamentally, what each of them required was a long and powerful list of WANTS. In the dead of night, when you are thousands of miles from home, the temperature is -30°F and every fibre of your being is begging to go home, what separates those who keep going from those who give up? The answer – a powerful-enough 'WHY?'.

Knowing what they wanted and, above all, stood to gain from completing the event was the only way I could be sure our challengers would make it to the finish. Once they'd done with telling me how much they were enjoying/hating the training and anticipating/dreading the race, I invited each of the challengers to create two lists.

List A provided answers to a critical question:

What will I gain if I succeed?
The list had to dig very deep. It had to touch an emotional chord in each participant. Some of the answers included:

I will make my family proud
It will improve my self-esteem
If I can do this, I can do anything
I'll be ready to move on to the next stage in my life
It will be my biggest achievement
I will know I'm unstoppable

Then we drew up a List B for:

What will I lose if I fail?
This time, the answers included:

I will look a prat on TV
My kids will be ashamed
I'll have let everyone down
I will feel a failure
I will lose faith in myself
I may never get over it

I needed the contestants on *The Challenge* to be fully aware of the consequences of success and, *especially*, of failure. The object of the exercise was to put the lists firmly in the forefront of their minds, providing such powerful motivation that they would do anything but stop.

When they returned to the UK, several challengers rang to thank me. We talked about their darkest moments when the urge to surrender appeared completely overwhelming. All confirmed that what kept them going was their lists – remembering what they stood to gain or to lose.

By the way, either list will do. We humans drift between the twin shores of pain and pleasure our entire lives. Some of us are motivated by the rewards of potential success, others by avoiding the trauma of failure. Few need both. It's an important point. Our man up Everest succumbed to altitude sickness but was reluctant to come down. It was only a one-to-one with me on a mobile-phone link from London to Nepal that enabled him to realise he'd already gained everything he set out to accomplish. He was focused on the wrong list.

Fuel in the tank Go back to your list of wants. My wish is for you to have such an overpowering determination to bring them about that not getting what you want is simply unthinkable.

On a clean sheet of paper, write down any want that particularly stands out. Then, follow what worked for *The Challenge* competitors. Divide the page in two. At the top of the left-hand column, enter the heading:

What Will I Gain If I Succeed?
You should, after this exercise, be left in no doubt at all that the goal is worth having. Make the list as long and powerful as you can. Make it exciting, powerful and compulsive.

On the right-hand side of the page, write the other heading:

What Will I Lose If I Fail?
This one should hurt. Really hurt. Hurt like hell! The mere idea of having to do without this want that you crave so strongly should leave you feeling deflated, depressed and *extremely* resolute that you are NOT going to fail. The better your list, the more it will hammer that home.

These lists are about *consequences*. Most of the consequences of our actions reach out and bite us long after it's too late to do anything about them. Whoever coined the phrase 'If I knew then what I know now,' was thinking about consequences.

Now, select whichever list – the joy of success or the grim despair of failure – is most powerful for you. Type it into your PC and convert it into the biggest document that you can, or write it out in huge letters with a marker pen on the largest sheet of paper you can find.

Print out, or photocopy, five or six copies and hang them on the walls of your house. Put them in the bedroom, the bathroom, the kitchen. Make them one of the first things you see in the morning and virtually the last thing you look at before turning in.

> This is your emotional fuel.
> Put enough of it in your tank and nothing on earth can stop you.

One of the contestants in *The Challenge* was the father of a six-week-old baby. He had to leave his new-born son to spend fifteen days trekking across the North Pole in temperatures that would drop to -60°F. The terrain was so hostile that one of the other competitors was airlifted to safety with frostbite of the penis! My contestant hated the cold, he was scared of dying and he missed his son every minute of the day.

His team won the race. If he can do it, so can you. But you have to *WANT* it badly enough. What do you have to gain? What do you stand to lose? Start making those lists.

QUESTION 2: WHY DO YOU WANT IT?
I know what you're thinking. Daft question. At first glance, I might even agree. You want what you want because . . . well, it's obvious. Everyone wants pots of money, to have rampant sex with the object of their lust, to be a Star of Stage, Screen and Reality TV. OK, maybe not Reality TV. BUT – you are not everyone, and what you want is unique.

Take another look at the top item on your want list. Ask yourself why you want what you've written down. If the answer happens to be 'To make twenty million pounds', ask yourself why you want *that*? Sure, the reasons might include 'To treat my family to the holiday of a lifetime . . . pay off my debts . . . buy a racehorse' etc. – but, I guarantee, surprises lie in store.

Well done. Now, carry on and ask yourself WHY you want THOSE THINGS? Suddenly, the answers become a lot more profound. These may include 'I will have the chance to travel . . . to give me the opportunity to find out who I am . . . to really take care of those I love'.

Dig deeper once again. *WHY do you want THOSE EXPERIENCES?* Prepare to uncover some timeless human needs (e.g.) – 'Then I'll feel glad to be alive,' or 'It will make me proud to be me.' THESE are your true ambitions or goals. Not only is twenty million pounds just a means to that end, but having a fat bank account without those qualities in your life will not lead to happiness. What it *will* produce is a sense of guilt at not being happy with all that cash while the rest of the world is starving etc., etc.

The key to achievement in life is a powerful 'WHY'. It's that 'WHY' that will take you exactly where you always intended to go.

QUESTION 3: HOW WILL LIFE BE *DIFFERENT* . . . WHEN YOUR WANTS COME ABOUT?

The key word here is *different*. Notice I do not use the words 'reborn', 'reinvented' or 'unrecognisable'. My work is not about encouraging clients to pursue fantasies so far beyond the horizons of their present existence that they border on the delusional.

Achievement – real, lasting, meaningful achievement – is about taking the skills and qualities you already have and using them as the foundation for a life that makes sense *to you*. If you want to marry Prince William, teach humans to fly or travel back in time, I wish you all the luck you surely will need. (And the urgent attention of a clinical psychiatrist.)

I deal with real people seeking real solutions to real problems. Real people create achievement by pursuing goals that take them far beyond their comfort zone yet feel sufficiently attainable that *they can sense their possibility*.

A brief recap:

- You know what you want.
- You know why you want it.
- The next step is to know, *to feel deep down*, what life will be like when you get it.

This is always a highlight. Watching people begin to access the life they desire is magical. Seeing the joy pulsating through every fibre of their being, observing energy levels soar through the roof, watching them come alive as the fire returns to their eyes – this is precisely what gives ME the passion for the work that I do.

Here's how it works.

a) Pick one desire from your list.
b) Find a quiet place and close your eyes.
c) *Take your time*. Now, very slowly, little by little, paint a picture in your mind of what life will be like once that want has materialised. Take at least two minutes for the picture to emerge.
d) Next, instead of watching the picture from the viewpoint of a spectator, step inside the body of the future you. See everything that is going on around you – where you are, who is with you, what is going on. Breathe in the richness of this magical life waiting to be lived.
e) Still running the movie in your mind, listen carefully to all the sounds that surround you. Is anyone speaking? Are there birds or other animals present – or is it just you and a glorious state of inner tranquillity?
f) This is the most important part of all. Feel the wonderful emotions of pleasure coursing through your body now your want has come to pass. How do you feel? Ecstatic? . . . satisfied? . . .

    content? . . . overjoyed? Soak up all these
    wonderful sensations and stay with them for at
    least 60 seconds.

g) Repeat steps a) to f) with one other want on your
    list.

Congratulations. If you have completed the process with application and focus, you will have a deep sense of the life that awaits you. You will feel energised, dynamic, positive and raring to go. You will know that your dreams make sense, your goals are realistic and a magnificent future waits to be grasped.

Fighting your demons

The exercises that you've just completed change lives. It may be that you need to ponder the information you've gleaned and outcomes you've reached for a few days, maybe a few weeks. Make that days. We've got a lot to do and momentum is critical. However, such revelations may be a lot to take in. You need to absorb them and feel comfortable with the journey we're undertaking.

It is usually about now that *self-esteem* issues appear. Most people suffer from appalling self-esteem. Such people include Presidents, the Chairmen of major corporations and international sporting legends. Self-esteem and self-confidence are entirely unrelated. As I pointed out during Session 1, self-confidence is a relationship of trust between 'you' and 'you', it is about knowing you can rely on yourself in times of stress or challenge.

Self-confidence can be increased through money or power or achievement. It can also be faked by astute use of tone of voice or body language.

Self-esteem runs deeper. Self-esteem is the extent to which you admire, appreciate and take care of yourself. This is not about vanity or narcissism. Standing in front of a mirror for hours will have no impact at all upon your self-esteem. This is about self-worth, a deep-rooted sense of personal integrity and value. Self-esteem cannot be faked. You cannot lie to yourself – at least, not about this.

The work you've done so far provides a head-on challenge to people suffering from low self-esteem. At long last, they know what they really want. They know it will happen if they let go of the fear. They are excited about what life will be like when it does. Yet something is holding them back. That something is low self-esteem. They start telling themselves that 'Nothing ever works out', 'It's all just a dream' or 'Who am I kidding?' They start thinking about past failures and dwelling on previous disappointments. It doesn't take long before the pulse of anticipation begins to become faint. We cannot let that happen. You fail, I fail – it's as simple as that. And failure is not what I am about.

Entire books have been written on self-esteem. Scan the Internet and you'll find hundreds of courses dedicated to the subject. Some trainers make a good living focused on nothing else but most of them start from entirely the wrong place. They talk about boosting baseline confidence, acknowledging the uniqueness of self and recognising one's divinity. Let me be blunt:

most people don't know where the baseline starts, they scoff at the notion that they are unique and react with horror to any suggestion that they may be divine.

Building self-esteem needs to start by recognising where you've come from. That place is often ugly, fraught with disaster and seasoned with a generous helping of trauma. Only by facing up to these issues and coming out on the other side can meaningful self-esteem begin to take root.

I call the following process 'Laying Down the Law' and we'll go through it in three stages. The objective is to empty your soul of all the emotional detritus that has been stored up for decades and let go of the harm you think you might have done to yourself. The intention is to create a space in which we can place something positive. This is not to be rushed. Take your time. At the risk of labouring the point, only by building rock-solid foundations can we construct a meaningful edifice for your life. It is time to forge a brand-new construction.

STAGE 1: THE CASE FOR THE PROSECUTION
I want you to take three sheets of paper. At the top of each page, write one of the following headings:

What I Dislike Myself For
What I Blame Myself For
What I Will Never Forgive Myself For

Spread the pages out – and start making those lists. This can be an extremely emotional process. Some people write nothing for several minutes, struggling to know where to begin. Once they do, the dam will often burst, and they may not know how to stop. Get it all down. Write even if – especially if – you feel tearful. Write until you get cramp, write until you are purged. How will you know when to stop? When you start to feel a quiet shift. In part, this shift is puzzlement – surprise at an unfamiliar sense of space – but with a tinge of peace. You may find you enjoy it. This part of the process is extremely cathartic. Simply shifting the lists from inside your wounded soul onto a sheet of paper is deeply soothing.

Look through your lists once more. Have you left anything out? Remember your childhood, school days, family members, long-lost uncles or cousins, friends, acquaintances, boyfriends, girlfriends, lovers, ex-wives. Trawl through your memory until every insult, rejection, disagreement, grudge, irritation and setback has been written down.

STAGE 2: THE CASE FOR THE DEFENCE

As you now know, I used to be a barrister. The primary role of counsel for the defence is to argue the case for the accused. In this instance, that happens to be you. Yes, that's you in the dock. Your case is about to be heard. In front of the Clerk of the Court is a charge sheet containing some or all of the items on the lists you've just drawn up.

Look around and you'll see there is no Prosecution Counsel. None is necessary. For longer than can you possibly remember, you have been your own Prosecuting Counsel. How many times have you told yourself you're

not good enough, berated yourself for under achievement or reminded yourself that it's all self-inflicted? We
should be grateful that all judges and juries are not like
you. The accused would always go down for life with
no hope of remand.

Imagine you could hire the best defence lawyer in
the world. Who would it be? Very few people are
acquainted with the names of leading lawyers so we'll
choose someone who is much better qualified, anyway.

I want you to think of someone who loves you.
Genuinely loves you. Please don't confuse feelings with
duty. It might be a lover, a parent, a business partner
or your best friend. Who do you know who always
has your best interests at heart? It doesn't matter if
they are still in your life or you haven't seen them for
years. They are, and will always be, special to you.

Picture them now. What are they wearing? How
pleased do you feel to see them? How pleased are they
to see you? Hear the sound of their voice as you greet
them. Put your arms around them and feel the deep
love in their embrace. Stay with that sensation for as
long as you like (no, that was too fast!).

Choose one of the items on your lists of charges.
Pick one that causes deep discomfort whenever it crosses
your mind. The court is now in session. Your friend
has come to argue on your behalf and is ready to make
a powerful case for your acquittal. Close your eyes.
Instead of looking on from the sidelines, step inside
the courtroom. Be there.

You see yourself in the dock, waiting to be judged.
Look at yourself with deep and heartfelt compassion.

Now – slowly – step into the body of that special person who loves you and is here to act as your lawyer. Know they will do a fantastic job in your defence. When he or she is ready, have your 'lawyer' argue the strongest case they possibly can. I want you to see things from the perspective of your lawyer: look out through his or her eyes at yourself in the dock. Imagine all the arguments that are being put forward in your defence. Some of these might include:

- What pressures were you under or subject to at the time?
- Were you too young or inexperienced to have behaved any differently?
- What were the reasons for acting in the way that you did?
- Was what happened really your fault?
- What allowances could have been made?
- Were others who were hurt really as affected as you thought? How were they responsible? Could they have behaved differently?
- Explain why the court should show compassion on your behalf.
- Provide the strongest possible justification for giving yourself a break.

I have created this LAW acronym to help you remember the process:

L – listen to the evidence with an unprejudiced ear. Some of the arguments will either be entirely new or put forward in a way you've never heard before. Trust me. However odd it may seem at first, when you adopt the mindset of someone who is completely on your side, you will discover a whole new way of looking at things.

A – allow your memories of the incident to be swayed in the light of new information.

W – weigh up all the evidence and come to a verdict.

Your 'advocate' need not restrict themselves to one charge. Which other complaints or accusations on the lists could be covered by similar arguments? What burdens need you no longer carry around? What else can be laid to rest today?

STAGE 3: FORGIVENESS
The defence has done a outstanding job. You have a whole new perspective on events that have held you back for so long – and you are finally ready to turn over a new leaf.

Just one more step and the slate is wiped clean. Take another sheet of paper and write in big, bold letters:

I am now willing to forgive myself for

★

★

★

★

Let your pen flow. You should find that your hand is struggling to keep up with the flood of ideas pouring from your mind. Keep writing, keep writing, keep writing. Your conscience is being salved. Long-standing emotional scars are being healed, feelings of blame, resentment and stress have begun to ebb away. Depending on the length of your lists, it may not be appropriate to cover all the 'charges' in a single session. This is fine. You can reconvene the court at any time that you choose, inviting different advocates to represent you when different cases are heard.

It's been a phenomenal session. Clients tell me they often go for a walk or sit in the car for a few minutes before driving away to absorb what they've learned. Personally, I never go from one session straight into the next. The impact can sometimes be as powerful for the coach as the client. I trust you are beginning to grasp the depth of our work. I hope you are feeling positive, energised and connected. I trust you are impatient to continue.

Not just yet. Now is a time to relax. Treat yourself to some wine, to a meal, a massage, a movie. Celebrate your discoveries so far. The journey to your dreams has begun.

Session Summary

1. **Answer these questions:**
   i) What do I want to do? – professionally, personally, financially and emotionally
   ii) What would you do if you weren't afraid?
   iii) What would you do if you knew you couldn't fail?

2. **Pick your top 3 wants. Determine beyond doubt:**
   i) What will you gain if you succeed?
   ii) What will you lose if you don't?

3. **Answer these questions:**
   i) Why do you want this? Dig down until you reach a fundamental truth.
   ii) How will life be different when you get it? Run your movie.

4. **Release the guilt:**
   a) Appoint your barrister.
   b) Hear the case for the defence.
   c) Reach a not-guilty verdict.

SESSION 3
Making It Happen

Nick is one of the most extraordinary people I have ever met. He is a natural achiever, dynamic, passionate, accomplished and gifted. Not only is he a self-made multi-millionaire but he is also happily married with four kids. A powerful public speaker and inspirational boss, Nick was also sufficiently talented to have made the grade as a professional tennis player.

The reason his life took a different course is that Nick has always loved interior design. Walking into an unfurnished room with Nick is an experience. He can see (and I mean *see*) curtains, cupboards, mirrors, light fittings, paintings and ornaments. He can match wallpaper that isn't there to carpets that haven't been laid. He is a master of his craft.

The property boom of the eighties was good to Nick. He earned enough to buy his first house and went into partnership with two other young bucks in the property industry. Then came the crash. Nick lost everything. He lost his house, his car, his stereo. He even had to resign from the tennis club.

More significant is what Nick did NOT lose. He did not lose his ambition, his grit, his self-belief. In order to support his wife and two baby girls, Nick took a job selling mobile phones. He was, true to form, the best salesman in the entire company. As soon as he'd saved up enough commission, Nick took his family to Turkey on holiday. It wasn't what they were used to. Instead of five-star luxury and en suite chambermaids, this was self-catering and making your own beds.

One afternoon, Nick got up from the pool and strode back to their apartment. Extracting a pen and sheet of paper from his case, Nick started to write. Four hours later, Nick had compiled:

- A list of his goals for the next 12 months.
- A list of his goals for the next 3 years.
- A list of his goals for the next 10 years.
- Why he deserved them.
- What he'd give back when he got them.
- What life would be like when he got them.
- A list of obstacles that would have to be overcome.
- A list of skills he would need to obtain.
- A list of every person he knew.

Nick made a plan. By the time he and his wife went out that evening, Nick had a vision. He knew how much money he would make and by when. He knew what kind of house the family would own 10 years on and how many rooms it would have. He knew what make of car he would drive, how many people his company would employ and what he would do for recreation.

Nick also made a list of resources. Most people in his financial situation would have claimed they didn't have any. Nick catalogued his physical attributes (health, strength, fitness), psychological resources (determination, resilience, guts) and personal qualities (charm, creativity, communication skills).

At dinner that night, Nick shared his vision with his wife. Not all of it – just enough to receive the emotional support for the journey he was about to embark on. Nick stuck to the plan and realised his aims well ahead of schedule:

- His 12-month goals were achieved in 8 months.
- All of the 3-year goals were completed in 2 years.
- The 10-year plan was accomplished in 6½ – with enough time left over to go back and reset the bar higher still.

Nick now lives in a double-fronted house in one of the most exclusive roads in Wiltshire (complete with pool and tennis court). The kids go to private school, the family enjoys four luxury holidays each year and he gives – as he promised he would – a fortune to charity.

Nick keeps that original plan on display in his office. It reminds him of how far he has come. It reminds him of what can be accomplished if you commit. It reminds all who see it that, no matter how distant they may appear, their dreams are still within reach. Let us briefly recap. In Session 2, you described what you want. Go back and look at your list. Are you sure you still want what you wrote down? Are you *certain*? Living in True Self changes everything. It changes your mindset, it transforms your world view, it may even have *redefined your ambitions*.

Our desires are no accident. They are emphatically a product of our personalities, our instincts and our spiritual connections. That combination is as unique as our DNA. Although others may insist they have your best interests at heart, no one outside the confines of your skin has the key to your combination. Before setting out to achieve them, be sure your desires are *yours*.

I trust you are completing the Animal Position exercise at least once per day. If not, stop and do it now. Resist any temptation to keep reading on the grounds of 'What the hell, I've got this far, I'll plough on anyway,' until you have a real sense of 'living in animal'. Once again – how can you have any idea what you want until you know who you are?

This chapter describes how to bring your deepest desires to life.

This chapter is about turning your wants into goals.

Do goals really matter?

Why set goals in the first place? Why not just float downstream on the Lilo of Life and 'go with the flow'? The answer is that goals are a fundamental ingredient for success because they create a map for the journey. If you have no idea where you are heading, how are you going to get there?

Goals function like your very own satellite-navigation system. Whenever you take a wrong turn, they guide you back in the right direction.

> Goals, particularly those that are written down,
> possess an explosive power to bring dreams to life.

Nowhere was this better illustrated than among students at Yale University in Connecticut, USA during the early fifties. At the request of their Governing Body, the students were invited to fill in a survey that stretched to well over two hundred pages.

Redefining the word 'exhaustive', the survey covered everything from their views on education to political attitudes. About the only thing it didn't cover was sex. Someone called Kinsey was doing that already.

Hidden away in an unobtrusive corner of the survey was a segment on goals. No one paid much attention to it at the time. The seemingly innocuous section simply asked whether each candidate had:

a) set out goals for their future
b) written them down.

And that was that. The questionnaires went back into a cupboard for twenty-five years and gathered dust on some very large shelves.

In the mid-seventies, someone at Yale remembered the survey. For the sake of completion, the Governing Body commissioned a follow-up report, contacting the (now middle-aged) students to see how they had got on. The results had the force of a nuclear explosion.

Analysts found that the 10% of students who had set

goals for themselves were more financially successful than the other 90% put together.

Then came the real revelation. Only 3% of the students had written their goals down. This tiny minority had acquired TEN TIMES greater wealth than the other 97% put together. These same students were also healthier, happier and far more fulfilled in their relationship with their partners. **And you are still wondering why to set goals!!!**

Writing goals down – and revisiting them at six-monthly intervals – enables my clients to set their mental compasses and recognise the knowledge, resources and skills they will need to fulfil their deepest desires. Having a map allows progress to be measured and ensures you are headed in the right direction. Everything that is not identified as a goal is exposed as a distraction.

Don't get me wrong, I am a staunch advocate of 'going with the flow'. I also encourage my clients to listen to their intuition (see Session 8) and avoid resisting where life wants to take them. However, to cut a long story short, universal intelligence (some say God, but let's not go there) is an invisible force that provides the ideal outcome for each and every event in our lives. Universal intelligence is particularly effective when we get out of the damn way – in other words, 'go with the flow'. However, universal intelligence can only go so far. Laze in bed from dawn to dusk and universal intelligence may have limited scope for impact (unless, of course, your long-term goal is to perfect the art of lying in bed). Many other books have been written on universal intelligence – Wayne Dyer is particularly eloquent on this subject – and I strongly recommend further investigation.

Putting flesh on the bones of your dreams takes careful planning and I use a variety of different techniques. The rest of this chapter provides two very distinct examples, one of which I employed with a professional sportsman and the other with a businesswoman seeking a brand-new career. Please don't regard these methods as mutually exclusive. You can apply either to any sort of goal.

Don't just read, DO IT YOURSELF! Once you've got to the end of this session, pick the approach that feels right for you and get down to work.

Even the greats get it wrong

In the winter of 2004, I took a call from an international rugby star. He wasn't sure if he needed a sports psychologist but most of the top players seemed to have one. It probably wouldn't do any good but he'd give it a go. How could I refuse?

Before we met, I watched him play. After spending so long working in football, attending a rugby match came as quite a culture shock. Walking through the turnstiles, I could scarcely believe my eyes. Both sets of fans were standing at the bar drinking – *with each other*!

In fairness, there was plenty of violence, far more than you'd ever see at a football game, but it was all on the pitch and the referee didn't seem concerned. He was far more preoccupied with not getting squashed in a scrum than telling a 6 ft 8 in lock forward to keep his fists to himself.

My client was playing for arguably the best club side

in the world. He was such a valued member of the team that they didn't even have a reserve in his position. However, his body language told me all I needed to know. He was clearly disenchanted, demotivated and had little idea of why he was playing.

Our initial session was intended to be informal, so we agreed to meet in the bar of one of London's top hotels. From the sidelong glances that came our way, several of the patrons clearly recognised my client. There was more Nudge Nudge, Wink Winking going on than in any sketch of *Monty Python's Flying Circus*.

Don't be deceived by what you've heard about sportsmen. They are far brighter than their tabloid reputation. Premiership footballers might not be familiar with the *Collected Works of Karl Marx and Frederick Engels* but can memorise every clause in their contracts (especially the ones about bonuses).

Rugger stars are brighter still. Many have enjoyed the (dubious) benefits of a public-school education and my new client was no exception. The World Cup was over and he'd spent months recovering from injury. In fact, he always seemed to be injured. And when he wasn't injured, he was thinking about how not to get injured.

Once we'd dispensed with the niceties, I gave him my opinion. I told him that rugby is a game for gladiators. Broken bones, dislocated shoulders and cauliflower ears are all part of the deal. Most mortals would barely survive the first tackle, but competing at the top of the sport demands absolute physical and psychological resilience. Above all, there is no such thing as

99% commitment. It has to be all or nothing. The attitude has to be 'welcome to the war'.

My client grinned. I breathed a sigh of relief. Would-be sports psychologists out there, please take note. At no point in your training will you be given any guidance on how to read the Riot Act to a man who is three times your size.

I set about reframing his mental approach towards injury. The essence of the work was to shift his focus from not getting injured to staying fit. We moved from 'What I don't want' to 'What I do want'.

The impact was immediate. Team-mates instantly observed a man playing with less fear in training. The following weekend, he laid on two tries in a big Cup game. After the match, I received an upbeat text message confirming a dramatic improvement in flair, creativity and enjoyment. As I expected, the message also said he wasn't sure if this had anything to do with our session. Still, we arranged to meet up again. After all, and I quote the man himself – 'What harm could it do?'

I duly trekked to his home in South London where I asked what he wanted me to help him achieve. The extended silence was all I needed to know. This world-class sportsman didn't know what he wanted. In fact, he had no goals at all.

Before we got down to goal setting, we went back a couple of stages and I explained the distinction between True and False Self. He got it immediately. The difference in performance between his last two games provided the perfect illustration.

We went through exactly the same process that you

experienced for yourself in Session 1. Listening to the national anthem while representing his country for the first time was the moment when he'd stood in True Self. The adjectives came thick and fast – buzzing, happy, passionate, energetic, fast, skilful, confident, focused and free. Simply listing the qualities of True Self was relighting the fire of intensity in his eyes.

His choice of animal was no surprise at all. The lion is the creature of many born leaders. The King of the Jungle is a killer, a predator and master of all it surveys. My client had been a leader in the dressing room, roaring at team-mates who failed to perform. He'd lost the pride in more senses than one.

Mention of False Self was met with a grimace. In this place, he was frustrated, anxious, tired, sore and uninterested. His only ambition was to get through games, to survive eighty minutes without sustaining too many injuries.

His False Self creature was a lazy cat, an overweight feline surviving on reflexes and the odd mouse (i.e. smaller opponents).

'What would the lion do with the mouse?' I asked.

'Eat it alive,' he laughed.

Back inside his own skin, the lion could begin to look forward. Instead of responding with stony silence, mention of life-goals was met with a list. Out they poured. He wanted to reclaim his place in the national side, to win the championship with his club team, to be selected to tour with his country the following summer, and to extend his career by three more years. Now we were getting somewhere.

Then a frown appeared as reality dawned. Present levels of inconsistency would deliver none of those goals; a significant improvement would be needed across the board. Time to get on with the work.

Creating a plan for success

STEP 1
This is all about goal setting and begins with a stock-take.
'What level of your potential are you performing to now?' was my opening question.

He didn't even blink. 'On a good day – 60%. No wonder I'm not enjoying my rugby.'

I then asked what figure would be needed to achieve the goals he'd outlined.

'At least 85%,' was the rueful reply. 'That's a heck of a jump from where I am now.'

STEP 2
This demands breaking a task down into individual elements in order to pinpoint the areas in greatest need of attention.
Rugby comprises a number of key skills – e.g. passing, tackling, running, goal kicking, line-outs. Each of these was accorded a percentage for current levels of perform-ance and a figure that would deliver all the goals on the list. My notes from the session recall that:

- passing skills needed to improve from 70% to 90%

- tackling to advance from 65% to 80%
- support play to develop from 55% to 85%
- running with the ball to move up from 50% to 75%.

'That should get me where I need to be.' He nodded. 'The question is how?' I was coming to that.

STEP 3
This is subtle; it's all about locating the difference that will make all the difference.
In the case of a top-class performer on the rugby field, improved passing skills are born of greater hand speed and superior decision making. Excellence in the line-out demands timing and anticipation while goal-kicking is about preparation and routine. Fine-tuning these components would provide incremental but crucial improvements.

STEP 4
This one demands taking each of the key skills in turn and isolating ways of delivering percentage upgrades.
I asked how a 15% improvement in tackling skills might be achieved. The answers he gave me included detailed analysis of technique on video, putting in extra hours on the barbells and one-to-one sessions after training.

We repeated the process for passing, tackling and set plays. It was all clearly do-able.

STEP 5

This is the nuts and bolts of the process. Having gathered details of what was required, we turned them into a To Do list.

This schedule of tasks can seem intimidating at first. Writing down all that you need to do might make you decide you don't want to do it. The human appetite for ploughing up and down a pool for 40 hours per week or beating the Bejesus out of 3000 golf balls or cycling hundreds of miles on godforsaken roads is not without limits. If it seems daunting, turn back to the exercise in **Session 2**. Ask yourself, 'Why do I want this? What will I get? What will I lose if I don't? **Is the payoff worth the price?'**

There were no such problems with this client. Failure would cost his living, his hard-earned reputation and status as an elite athlete. He was seriously hungry. We drew up a list. It *was* a long one. Completing all the tasks would require total dedication plus considerable backing from coaches, team-mates and family. He promised to get on the mobile as soon as I left.

STEP 6

This will ramp up desire with that tantalising question – 'When I get what I want, how will life be different?'
Some of his answers were painfully honest. 'I won't be such a pain in the arse,' was one. 'I will be able to look myself in the mirror,' was another. Others included, 'I'll win back the respect of my team-mates and the fans,' and 'I'll look forward to reading about myself in the papers again.'

STEP 7

This is the one that bolts the vision into place by adding a 'When'. Without timeframes and deadlines, discipline soon goes missing.

It didn't take long. We returned to the To Do list and assigned dates to each task. I kept a list of these for myself. None of my clients is in the slightest doubt that I'll be on their case at the first sign of slacking.

STEP 8

This one adds definition to the timeline.

Assuming all the tasks on the To Do list will be accomplished, what would my client commit to accomplishing in:

- 1 week from now
- 1 month
- 3 months
- 6 months
- 1 year

I could tell we were done. As his eyes flicked through the notes that I'd made, his jaw was set in utter resolution.

I know what you're thinking – 'How well did he do?' In no particular order:

a) his club went on to land the Cup and League double
b) after discussions with the coach, another player

    was recruited in his position to share the
    workload

c) my client was recalled to the international arena

d) he was picked to tour in the summer – but
    turned down the invitation to give his body time
    to recuperate

e) he no longer stresses about injury.

He even got me tickets for the Cup Final. Two years later we're still working together and – what do you know? – he's *still not sure* about this sports psychology 'stuff'. Some people.

Setting goals for life

It was a glorious sunny day in September. I had just wound up a corporate-golf clinic when I was approached by one of the players. Her day had not gone as expected. The overworked MD of a City PR company, she'd turned up late, rushed out to the range, missed my entire introduction yet learned enough in fifteen minutes to play the best golf of her life.

'I've got to know how you did that,' she beamed. 'Let me in on the secret.' I felt like Derren Brown. After divulging one or two nuggets, I tucked into my salad and listened to her story. This incredibly skilled, phenomenally bright individual had started to question her professional integrity.

In the early days, her company maintained a policy of only taking on clients that offered stimulating projects and were fun to work with – or else expanded their range of professional skills. 'Now, we'll take anyone who can afford the fees,' she confessed. 'I don't know why I do what I do any more. I don't even know why we're in business.'

I have been invited to work with a number of senior executives in household-name public limited companies, and I hear the same story time and again. Many of these people are already set for life and require deeper motivation than mere financial reward. Some run their companies for the sake of their staff. Others do so for the good of their customers or the community. Some work themselves into an early grave for the benefit of their shareholders. The sense of disenchantment that I see at the top of UK corporations is overwhelming. Strictly 'off the record' (e.g. over lunch and after the fourth glass of Chablis), the blame is heaped on the unceasing pressure of trying to increase half-yearly profits to please City analysts.

Decent people find themselves taking indecent decisions – closing plant or stores; laying off loyal members of staff – to stop the share price being marked down. While this discussion is clearly beyond the ambit of this book, the echo from one coaching session to the next is unmistakable. The talent drain from plcs to private-equity companies must be apparent to someone other than me.

Kate wanted out. She had long harboured a dream of opening her own chain of exclusive food stores. She asked me to coach her through the transition. We met three weeks later at her office. In the interim, I e-mailed Kate the process described in Session 1, we had a couple of sessions over the phone – and she was already transparently established in True Self.

The approach I took with Kate is by no means one I apply with all clients. It demands a playful personality, a vivid imagination and a willingness to make magic out of thin air. This exercise has its origins in dream work. The correct interpretation of dreams (most people have no idea, and jump to entirely the wrong conclusions) begins with an acceptance that everyone in your dreams – friend, foe, lover, mother, hero, Hitler – is, in fact, *you*. What dreams comprise are different aspects of an individual's personality that are playing out a drama among themselves and seeking resolution. I have applied this learning with stunning success in the fulfilment of goals.

Our session began with me asking Kate to paint a picture. 'What will the first store look like?' I inquired. 'Where will it be located? How many members of staff will you have? What kind of food will you sell?'

Kate told me she'd already got her eye on a site in West London – in Fulham, no less. Inspired by continental patisseries, Kate's shop would specialise in high-quality, additive-free, homemade bread and cakes. The shop would have two bakers, five shop assistants and be open from 5.30 a.m. until midnight. I allowed Kate to spend a few moments in the shop – she could almost *smell* the *pain au chocolat* – and then we moved on.

'What sort of person would run a shop like that?' I probed.

Kate looked puzzled. 'Whatever do you mean?' she asked.

I rephrased the question. 'What kind of person would be suited to running the store? For example, would it be a man or a woman?'

Kate went 'inside' for a moment. She pondered. A flash of inspiration appeared. 'A woman,' Kate declared.

'And how old would this woman be?' I pressed. 'Twenties, thirties, fifties, sixties?'

'Early forties,' Kate nodded. She herself was 36.

'What would this woman be called?' I wondered. This is always a key moment in the process. Either the client gives me an 'I've no idea what you're on about' look, or they do exactly what Kate did.

'Anna!' she giggled. 'Yes, Anna.' Kate was surprised and baffled but intrigued. She was eager to go on.

I needed a clearer picture of Anna. 'What kind of person are we talking about? Describe Anna to me.'

Kate hesitated a moment, gathered a picture in her mind and launched into a potted biography:

'Anna is smart, clever, capable and extremely hard working. She really loves people and understands that the shop isn't just a shop but part of a community. She isn't worried (by the way, *I couldn't have stopped Kate now if I'd wanted to*) about being undercut by local supermarkets because her customers would never buy their bread from Tesco's or Sainsbury's. She loves what she does but has a life outside the shop. She takes time out in her day to go for walks or meet friends and is always buying little gifts for staff to say thank you. She is smartly dressed, personable and, yes, happy.'

Kate had disappeared into her vision. She was completely relaxed, her breathing had slowed, even the colour of her cheeks had lightened. Kate had no idea what we were doing, only that she'd *connected*.

'What is Anna's mission in life?' I asked. Kate took a few moments before answering. Long enough to get back *under the skin* of her character.

'She is passionate about healthy food. Anna will not compromise on quality or service. Her mission is to create an experience that is so special that her bread becomes nothing less than a lifestyle choice for her customers.'

To the conscious mind, this is a baffling process. Kate had come up with a character she'd never met to run a store that didn't exist. She knew this character's name, could describe her personality and even 'Anna's' mission in life.

I brought Kate back to the room. 'Given all that you know about Anna,' I went on, 'what are the qualities she possesses that you need yourself?'

Kate smiled. 'I was thinking about that. Anna knows far more about food than I do. She is an expert on what separates great bread from, say, an average loaf. She knows her customers inside out. Anna is also better than me at reading a Balance Sheet!'

I was scribbling notes as fast as I could. Kate had isolated what she would require to step into Anna's shoes. This would include greater product knowledge, a deeper understanding of her customer base and solid accounting skills.

The next part can be challenging. Clearing a space on the table, I asked Kate to *draw her shop*. She hesitated for a nanosecond ('No one has asked me to draw anything since Sixth form') then rolled up her sleeves and began sketching. I had brought with me a large sheet of paper and some crayons. Kate's fingers were a blur of activity. She drew counters and ovens and doors and people and tables and pastries. *Kate glowed as she drew*.

My clients are not always blessed with artistic talent. I, myself, never graduated beyond matchstick men. I ask non-artistic clients to create a collage of their goal with images from newspapers and magazines. It is astounding how often random, seemingly unassociated images can give birth to a torrent of fresh ideas and new inspiration.

Drawing completed, the remaining stages were more prosaic. I asked Kate to make a list of the resources at her disposal. She was more fortunate than most. Financially independent (though not wealthy enough to open a chain of shops), Kate had a vast network of contacts from which to source a) additional backing, b) expert advice on the retail sector and c) instant PR. 'I might have to take one or two people to lunch,' she conceded. Sympathy from me was not forthcoming.

Kate could also call on the emotional support of her partner who had long been urging a change of career. 'I am young,' she reflected, pausing for effect, 'well – "ish". I'm energetic, intelligent, experienced in business and largely optimistic. And I've got you!' I tried not to blush.

It would not all be plain sailing. Reluctantly, Kate ticked a series of hurdles that would need to be overcome. For the first time in our session, Kate frowned.

She would have to hand in her resignation, resist the blandishments of a board that would undoubtedly try to persuade (i.e. bribe) her to stay, explain her decision to corporate colleagues and adjust to an entirely new lifestyle. 'It's a lot to take on,' she conceded. 'I need to be sure.'

In order to make certain she was, I asked Kate a question that will, by now, be familiar: 'What will you gain if you succeed?' The glow returned to Kate's face as she ticked off the list:

'Happiness, contentment, energy, satisfaction, pride, joy, a renewed sense of purpose, a feeling that life is worth living again. Not to mention not having to look smart all the time, sit through all those damn meetings or work with people who clearly don't want to work with me either. Is that enough?' I assured her it was.

We moved on to her To Do list. Starting a new business is a complex process and Kate's list took 45 minutes to complete. Sheets of paper were strewn all over the floor and she thought hard before arranging the jobs in order of priority. 'It's a lot of work,' she agreed, 'but at least I can see what needs to be done, by when and by whom. Mostly me, of course. Still, I now have a structure.'

We were nearly there. As with my rugby star, I asked Kate to write down how her goal would have advanced in:

- 1 month's time
- 3 months
- 6 months
- 1 year

Aided by that sequence, Kate constructed a chain linking each event to the one before and after. I like my clients to take immediate action. In order to provide even sharper focus, I asked Kate to consider:

1. how she would commit to advancing her goal one week from now.
2. what she would do to advance her goal *today*.

Kate promised to brainstorm a name for her business by the end of the day (she already had three to choose from). In seven days, the title would be registered at Companies House and a domain name purchased for the website.

The final 'step' applies to both processes – sport and business. If I'm honest, it's not really a step at all, more of an *aide-mémoire*. I strongly encourage my clients (i.e. boss them) into **celebrating** the fulfilment of each stage. This is about far more than having fun.

Most people set targets for themselves at some stage of their lives. Many of those targets – you *will* have plenty of examples of your own – were actually achieved. However, **neglecting to recognise our achievements means we soon forget they happened at all.** Our memories need *markers*. Unless you put these markers in place, then successes (*real* successes) are swiftly wiped from our hard drives.

When I point out their long list of achievements to clients with low self-esteem, the response I often get is 'Anyone could have done that', 'It really wasn't such a big deal' or (this one really makes me burn) 'I'd already moved on to something else.' **Success must be registered.** The more it is registered, the greater impact it will have. Treat yourself to a new piece of jewellery, a book, a CD, a meal out – it doesn't have to be anything expensive but acknowledging success has three major benefits:

1. It transforms self-perception. You gain emphatic proof that you are an achiever.
2. Success is a habit. Registering achievements reinforces that habit and sharpens the appetite for more.
3. Treating yourself is about self-esteem. L'Oréal were incredibly clever with their slogan 'Because I'm worth it'. Consumers bought expensive products – not for their intrinsic value, but because of what it told them about the way they felt about *themselves*.

Of course, treating yourself is also *fun*. Before setting out in pursuit of your goal, you may want to make a list of 10 gifts you will buy yourself **when you have accomplished each stage.** Make them prezzies that you'd really like but otherwise would make do without. **And make sure you stick to the bargain.** Remember, confidence is a state of trust between 'you and you' and that trust must not be betrayed.

Goals are rarely achieved without setbacks, heartache and moments when you wonder who the hell ever thought of this crazy idea. In moments of doubt, go back to your list of WHYs! If your WHYs lack conviction, come up with others, come up with as many as you can. Even better, *sit inside the experience*. Repeat the exercise in Session 2. Find a quiet place where you won't be disturbed and create a picture in your mind of what life will be like once your dream has materialised. *Don't just watch*. Step inside your body and soak up those fabulous feelings.

What a session this has been! You now stand in True Self, equipped with goals that come straight from the heart and a detailed plan to bring them to life. You know you can do it. I know you can do it. I know you *will*.

As I said at the start of this session, getting the life you want is not a spectator sport. An intellectual understanding of goal-setting processes achieves nothing. You have to do it. Read no further until you have.

Session Summary

1. Remember those Yale students and write down your goals.
   Would you have been one of the 3% or the 97%?
2. For each goal, apply the strategy for making it happen that suits you best. Use this as a reminder:
   a) Do a full stock-take of the current state of play.
   b) Determine status-quo/improvement percentages.
   c) Locate the difference that will make the difference.
   d) Form the plan that will achieve the difference.

e) Make a To Do list
f) Keep asking, 'When I get what I want, how will life be different?'
g) By when – add dates to the To Do list.
h) Fine-tune your 'Results' timeline including action to be taken *today*
i) Celebrate!

SESSION 4
I Believe I Can Fly

One of my lifelong convictions is that everyone on earth (priests, dentists, children) has something to teach me. The point was emphatically driven home by a conversation I had with the man who sells the *Big Issue* on our high street.

Charlie is in his late forties though he looks far older. Charlie has four teeth, holes in his trousers and a drink problem (which I wish he'd told me about before I gave him a bottle of sherry for Christmas). Anyway, Charlie has been through two marriages (he missed his first wife, the second could 'go to hell'), declared bankruptcy twice and is a fabulous observer of human nature.

Charlie can tell who is going to buy the *Big Issue* from fifty yards by their body language (it would be further but his eyesight is ropey). Charlie smiles when it rains and sings excerpts from musicals when the sun shines (mostly *Carousel*). Now that he has a roof over his head and money for smokes, Charlie is one of the happiest people I know.

Takings were down one morning when I stopped for a chat. To my surprise, Charlie was perky as ever.

'You should try being gloomy for a change,' I kidded. 'They say a pessimist is never disappointed.'

'That may be true,' smiled Charlie, 'but an optimist has a much happier life.'

While Charlie's words are burned into my memory, Albert Einstein put it better still: 'The most fundamental question you will ever ask yourself,' Einstein observed, 'is do I believe in a friendly or a hostile universe?' What Einstein is saying, and Charlie embodies, is that our state of mind is a choice – *and the choices we make become the life we create*.

Reality is a myth

In simple English, our lives are determined by what we tell ourselves to be true, even if it is not. Each of us manufactures our view of the world; we impose meaning (i.e. *our truth* – with the emphasis on '*our*') upon everything that happens. This means we have the option to change it at any time.

The truth is not what it seems. It is a moveable object. Most of us can recall an experience of seeing precisely the same event with someone else but remembering what happened entirely differently. Reality is just our *interpretation*, no more and no less. The problems start when these interpretations acquire a power they were never intended to have. Then, interpretations become *our beliefs*.

Can you remember the first exam you ever sat? Mine was the dreaded 11-plus – the exam which, even at that tender age, could determine your educational fate. For months, rumours had been flying around the school. External examiners were monsters with horns, the questions were so hard you could barely read them and we were all stupid and going to fail. In fairness, there was plenty of evidence to support that last bit. Our teacher went to great lengths to emphasise that we were terminally thick and destined to end up sweeping floors.

One day in January, entirely without warning, the monsters arrived. We sat quaking at our desks trying not to pee and awaited our doom. Men in grey cardigans handed out the papers and told us we had two hours to determine the course of our lives (or that was how it appeared). Those who passed would go to a lovely school where the teachers were friendly, the classrooms were shiny and you got to play football with boys who were too nice to tackle you. A different fate awaited all who failed. They would be cast out into the wilds of the local comprehensive, forced to surrender their dinner money to the bullies, sit in classes with 45 other dimwits and spend hours in detention three times a week.

I'm not sure that much has changed. I watch aghast as my contemporaries put their kids (and themselves) through utter torment in the name of trying to get Geoffrey into 'the right school'. Looking back, I wonder why. There is absolutely no evidence that academic children grow up to lead happier, more productive and fulfilled lives.

A poll among my own ex-classmates is extremely revealing. Almost to a man (or woman), those who have achieved the greatest success in the eyes of the world were among *the least academic*. If school equipped them with anything at all, it was a sheer, bloody-minded determination to prove a point to those who had written them off. The real reason they 'made it' is equally clear. They found what they were good at and stuck to it. They discovered their niche, expanded their skills (in that specific field) and *focused*. Written off as numbskulls – because they did not conform to the narrow definition of 'clever' – they just went off and achieved.

I passed my 11-plus exam – not that I had any idea how. When the envelope dropped on the doormat, my mother opened the flap, beamed with approval and I was flavour of the month. But my beliefs about exams had been fixed. I *loathed* the buggers. They were painful, terrifying and had the power to send you to a place called 'rejection'. My passing them was a fluke, and I was destined to come a cropper in the fullness of time.

Payback came in the shape of my driving test. Driving was really *important*. Driving a car meant you were cool and didn't have to rely on your parents for lifts or meet girls for dates at bus stops. I failed three times (actually it might have been four, I lost count). *I was a really good driver*. The first test I failed was on a pure technicality. Oh all right, I was halfway over a zebra crossing in a traffic jam when some old biddy appeared on the passenger side and banged on the bumper with her walking stick. Apart from that, I did nothing wrong.

From that first test onwards, I knew I'd fail before I even turned up. The fact that instructors – my mother started teaching me but her nerves gave out – kept saying that passing was a mere formality made no difference at all. My mind was made up. I hated exams and they hated me. The way I eventually passed was by changing my mindset.

I was still sure that I'd fail *but decided not to care.* I made a conscious decision that driving didn't matter. I had no money to buy a car, anyway, so what difference would it make? I approached the next test in a state of total relaxation. There were *no consequences to failing* so I had nothing to lose.

I can still picture the moment the examiner told me I'd passed. We were sitting by a roadside in Mill Hill, North London, at ten to three on the afternoon of 20 October 1978. As was customary by now, I knew the verdict before it was given. 'I'm pleased to say that you've passed,' exhaled the examiner, in a tone that suggested he could not have cared less. I was incredulous. So was he. *I actually started arguing.*

'What do you mean I've passed?' I snapped. 'I drove exactly the same in all the other tests. Three years this has taken me, three years of suffering and humiliation and . . .' I was on a roll but he'd got out of the car. Even when I went inside to exchange my provisional licence for the real thing, I was still fuming. I could not accept that I'd passed. It took almost a week to sink in. *Passing an exam posed a challenge to my reality.*

The point I'd missed was that **my reality had changed.** It had changed because I'd reframed the underlying beliefs (e.g. 'Driving matters') that supported the structure of pessimism. Remove the beliefs and the structure collapses.

> Human beings create their own reality, and you can change your reality whenever you choose.
> Change your reality and you change your future.

The placebo effect

I was never a big fan of the TV series *M.A.S.H.* Major Burns was an idiot, Corporal Klinger was just plain annoying and Radar did the same thing every week. One episode, however, was stunning. The *M.A.S.H.* field hospital had just run out of sedatives when it was swamped with casualties from a Vietcong incursion. Hawkeye barely managed to patch up the wounded when night time fell. Desperate for sleep to provide temporary relief from their injuries, patients pleaded with Hawkeye for tranquillisers.

He had none to give them. After consulting a nurse (an attractive one, of course), Hawkeye decided to lie. He located a bottle of plain white tablets and told the patients that they were sleeping pills. Some got to sleep, others did not. Hawkeye went round a second time and handed another pill to those still awake. 'Be careful,' he counselled, 'these are particularly strong.' This time, they all drifted off.

Although this story was made for TV (yes, I *do* know), most doctors have dozens of similar tales based on real-life events. Placebos provide particularly graphic proof of the fact that human beings create their own reality. Scientific discovery adds weight to the argument. According to Heisenberg's Uncertainty Principle (bear with me, Reader), white-coated men of science should be able to plot the precise path of a particle, such as an electron, moving through space – but they can't. Something very odd happens when scientists try to measure an electron's position and momentum. They have discovered there is an *uncertainty* associated with each measurement. Whichever boffin tries to take such a measurement, each one records different results. The very act of measurement itself – and the actions of the person taking it – has an impact on what is being measured.

I know – what possible relevance does this have to you? Heisenberg's theory has enormous implications beyond the sterilised confines of the laboratory. If the old boy was correct – and, eighty years later, there is absolutely no evidence to suggest he was not – the way that an object behaves *depends who is observing and how they react to it*. If that is true at the level of electrons, how much more does it apply to human beings and their impact on the events of their lives?

It is your view of the universe that will govern your experience. If you believe that life is hard, it will be. If you believe that people are kind, they will be. If you believe that you are blessed, then you are. And the converse is equally true. *Human beings create their own reality*. Now, let's do something about yours.

Your beliefs can keep you in chains

Do you have elephant tendencies? I'm not a big fan of zoos. I know they do great things, and lots of species would be extinct without them, and where else could we see rare animals from the furthest flung corners of the globe? But the sight of animals behind bars gets my back up.

On the rare occasions I do go to the zoo (bored kids are usually involved), I love hanging out with the elephants. There is something particularly magisterial about this gigantic but gentle species that draws visitors to their compound.

In order to stop the elephants running off into the sunset, some zoos attach chains to their legs fixed to stakes in the ground. While this practice makes me long to find the nearest attendant and give them a slap, the chains are invariably quite small. In fact, on closer observation, the chains are decidedly flimsy and would barely restrain a large cow, let alone a creature weighing 7000 kilos, more than five tonnes. There has to be a logical explanation. And there is.

The chains are placed on the elephants *when they are babies*, striving and struggling for their freedom. You may have even seen the infants, tugging at the stakes with all the pitiful might they can muster. By the time they reach their first birthday, most elephants give up the fight. They 'know' they are tethered, go with the flow and waste no more energy on a struggle they have come to realise is futile. But the elephants are wrong!

A fully grown elephant could comfortably rip the stake from the ground and break free of its chains. Only their conditioning from infancy – their continuing *beliefs* – holds them back.

I'll ask you again. Do you have elephant tendencies?

THE POWER OF BELIEF

As we have seen, beliefs are just interpretations. Interpretations are theories and theories can be disproved. One of the main reasons that beliefs are so powerful is they bind together in clusters. In NLP language, these clusters are called 'hierarchies'. For example, one of your beliefs may be 'I never have any money.' Such a *belief* may appear to be innocuous but represents just the tip of the iceberg. Dig a little deeper and

'I never have any money,' becomes 'I am always broke.' What started out as a belief has become your *identity* – part of your description of 'who I am'. Dig deeper still and

'I am always broke,' becomes 'I will always be poor.' What started out as a belief has now become your *destiny*. Dig even deeper and

'I will always be poor,' becomes 'I am worthless.' Now you've sacrificed *self-esteem*.

Beliefs penetrate to the core of our being. What may seem to be mildly damaging may have far-reaching consequences, stripping individuals of the power of self-determination.

Disempowered people surrender responsibility for themselves.

Disempowered people make excuses instead of taking action.

Disempowered people give up.

THE NATURE OF BELIEFS

Not all beliefs are harmful. It is important to distinguish those that have got you this far from those that will get you no further. It is crucial to understand that *beliefs need not be permanent.* However, failing to get rid of beliefs you've outgrown will mean they keep holding you back.

Beliefs fall into two distinct categories – productive and limiting:

Productive beliefs are expansive. They generate confidence, ambition and motivation. Productive beliefs are like vitamins, they nourish, support and enrich everything that you do. They are empowering.

Limiting beliefs are restrictive. They keep you chained – like those elephants; they deplete, discourage and distress. They are usually initiated by some sort of fear but held in place long after the cause of that fear has subsided.

TAKING STOCK – START WITH THE POSITIVES

It is time for another stock-check. I want you to find out which of your beliefs serve you and which are blocking your path.

This next exercise will take 20 minutes. If you're strapped for time, two separate sessions of 10 minutes will be fine. Find yourself two sheets of paper. On the first sheet, please write the heading **Productive Beliefs.** Now brainstorm.

Productive beliefs about yourself may include:

I am strong
I am rich
I am a great cook

There is no one like me
I am beautiful
I am funny
I like myself
I am clever
I am lucky
I tell a good joke
I can hold an audience
People like me
I am a good cricketer
I am fearless
I make friends easily
I excel at my job
I am a good husband/wife/brother/parent
I am a good listener
I am trusted
I am loved

This exercise can be quite a stretch for many people. Everyone knows that praising yourself is a slippery slope that can lead to something nasty like . . . self-assurance – and we wouldn't want any of that nonsense, would we?

Take a reality check, please. This *is not boasting*. Reminding ourselves of our good points is not some 'Look at me!' ego trip (that's what sports cars are meant for) or a one-way ticket to Narcissism Central. This is a long-overdue inventory of all that stuff polite boys and girls have been taught not to tell themselves because 'If I do, no one will like me.'

Not true, is it? People already know all that stuff

about you and – guess what – that is part of *why* they like you. People want to be in the company of friends, colleagues or lovers who are talented and powerful and can bring out the best *in them*. Stop pretending to be smaller than you are, no one believes it except you anyway.

Has anyone ever droned on about how talented you are and what you could do with your life if you got off your backside and how they wish they had your gifts or talents or charm? Look at your list of productive beliefs. This is what they meant. Maybe they weren't just being nice! Feels good, doesn't it, to see your list in black and white? Powerful, impressive, reassuring. One other thing: these productive beliefs of yours are not on loan. You will not be giving them back.

'Tears before bedtime' syndrome Anyone who has ever been a child (doh!) will be familiar with the phrase 'tears before bedtime'. Junior goes to the fair or the circus and has a fabulous time and maybe presents or sweets are involved but then something happens and it all goes horribly wrong. What ensues will usually conform to the following pattern:

1. Junior throws up/has a tantrum/makes a spectacle of him/herself.
2. Mum and Dad vow never to let it happen again. 'That's the last time you ever . . .'
3. Junior learns that too much pleasure is 'dangerous'. He/she learns that filling their being to the brim with the joy of existence is risky.

'Tears before bedtime' is one of the inhibitors that keeps adults constrained. It is a form of learned behaviour that is accompanied by a painful lesson: hold yourself back – stay in your box.

> You are no longer a child.
> Being all that you can will not lead to tears before bedtime.
> Being less than you can most certainly will.

ROOT OUT THOSE NEGATIVES

It's time to nail your limiting beliefs. You know the drill. Take that other piece of paper and write the heading **Limiting Beliefs** at the top. If anything, I'd like you to spend even longer on this one. List the beliefs that you want to eradicate. Be brave, be honest, be thorough. Once you have got them all down, I will show you a technique that will consign your demons to history.

Limiting beliefs about yourself may include:

I am a failure
I cannot perform under pressure
I am unattractive
I cannot control my temper
I am accident-prone
I am useless at sport
I go red in the face
I will never be promoted
I will never learn to swim

I am weak
I have no friends
I am stupid
I am messy
I am a lousy dresser
I will never find a boyfriend
I cannot lose weight
I am no fun
I am a loser

Make sure your list is complete. Go back over it one more time. Is there anything else nagging away in the back of your brain that should really be included? Please add it now.

So there they are in all their glory – your limiting beliefs. And a fine mess they have got you into. What would life be like without them? What might you achieve if they were not holding you back? How would you like to be rid of them?

Let us start by putting them in order. Which of the beliefs on your list have caused you the greatest damage? Pick out the three main culprits and number them from 1 to 3. In the cold light of day, are these the three you would like to get rid of? Don't worry if you've got more than three. There will be plenty of time to work through them all.

How to change a limiting belief

1. *Pick a disempowering belief*
We'll start with the one at the top of your list. Write it down on a new page. Does it require further

refinement or a bit of extra clarity? You should be looking at a belief that is instantly recognisable, one you 'know' rather better than you'd like.

2. Substitute an empowering belief

The mind can't stand a vacuum. When you dispose of a limiting belief, it is crucial to put something else – something effective – in its place. At the simplest level, you can go for an 'opposite': e.g. *replace*

'I never make new friends,' *with* 'I make new friends very easily.'

A more resourceful option is to choose a replacement belief that will generate a whole new type of behaviour: e.g. *from* 'I am bad with my hands,' *to* 'I can fix anything.'

3. Think of three occasions when your empowering belief was true

'But it's never happened to me . . . There haven't *been* any such occasions . . . If it had happened three times, I wouldn't need this exercise.'

Stop arguing, I've heard it all before.

Supporting examples may take a bit of finding but can be spotted quite easily if you know what to look for. Let's take the empowering belief:

'I make new friends very easily.'

It may indeed be many years since you made a new friend but there will have been times when even the most solitary individual has managed to do so. Let your mind drift back gently to childhood. Who was your best friend in nursery or primary school? The fact that you haven't seen them for decades is absolutely immaterial. What about clubs you belonged to, teams you played for or someone whose interests you shared? How about secondary school, college or university? Who did you get along with during that period of your life?

Be flexible. The word 'friend' can have any number of different meanings from 'temporary acquaintance' to a member of your family. Nor is friendship necessarily governed by the length of time spent in each other's company; many of the most important people in our lives are just passing through.

4. *Run the movie*
What is your favourite cinema? It may be the local Multiplex or that fleapit where you spent Saturday mornings as a child watching Roy Rogers kill all those Injuns.

Imagine you are there now but have the entire cinema to yourself. The projectionist has loaded three special films – high-budget versions of your three supporting examples. Sit back in your seat and watch the first of those films now. Pick out all the detail you can as the curtain slides back and the scene unfolds. *Your film has begun.*

5. *First, watch the screen*
SEE yourself on the screen. See all the colours, the movement, the sequence of events as it happened. There's your friend! What was he or she wearing?

Where were you both? How old were you? What were you doing in this scene? What happened next? You will be amazed just how much information comes back as you sit back and watch. *No trying, please; just let it happen.*

HEAR all the sounds that are part the movie. Is anyone talking? What is being said? Hear the unique sound/tone/pitch/accent of the voice of your friend. Are there any noises in the background – if so, what are they? Is anyone else around and what are they saying?

FEEL all the pleasurable sensations that were part of that experience. It *was* great to be in the company of your friend. How did he or she make you feel – about your friendship or about yourself? How did having a friend like that make you feel about life in general? I want you to experience all those wonderful feelings again. Feel them strengthening all the time as they spread round your body. The movie has now finished. How good was it to live through that special time all over again? It's about to get better.

6. *Now, step into the picture*
Until now, you have remained *dissociated* – viewing the movie as a spectator, maintaining a clear distance between yourself and the screen. We are going to run the movie again. However, this time, I want you to *step inside your body*. When I do this exercise – and *I do it all the time* – I find it helps to feel myself moving from outside to inside the skin of 'that other person'. It's as if I am bringing the shadow to life, inhabiting its arms and legs and mind. I 'move in' and 'take over'.

The scene from the movie is the same as before. Though there may be subtle additions. As you start to live inside the experience, you may begin to notice one or two extra details – that the images are growing more vivid, the voices are clearer and the feelings are stronger. This should be, by some distance, the richer of the two movies. You are now *associated* with the experience.

The second clip is now ready and loaded in the projector but take a moment before it begins. Give yourself a few seconds to allow the impact of the first movie to really sink home. You should get a sense of 'OK, that's in there' before moving on.

7. *Repeat the process*
Now run the movies of your second and third supporting examples, using exactly the same process, i.e.:

1. Run the movie – see, hear and feel in the way I've described, but from the vantage point of a spectator.
2. Run the movie again, but step into the screen.

8. *Enjoy the results*
This exercise works on both a logical and a sub-conscious level. The left side of the brain has now discovered that your empowering belief is not just wishful thinking. You have provided hard evidence of three occasions when what you desired actually came about. It really *is* possible.

At a subconscious level, having three of those 'OK,

that's in there' moments leaves a deep impression on the right side of the brain. Resistance is reduced, the barriers are down.

The movies are over, the credits have rolled. Let's see if it worked. Return to the sheet of paper on which is written your empowering belief. How do you feel about it now?

Do not expect a 'Wow, that's amazing, this is the answer I've been waiting for all my life' kind of moment. What you should feel is settled. You may notice a heightened sense of solidity and feel, intuitively, that your empowering belief is now in place and ready to add substance to your future.

In the absence of this feeling, a little more work needs to be done. If you are struggling, the most likely explanation is that one of your supporting examples (of a successfully realised empowering belief) failed to ring true. Perhaps it wasn't strong enough, or it didn't evoke the right kind of memories, or else it simply didn't have enough juice. Go back and pick something else. Find a moment – it does only have to be a moment – that gets the job done. **I promise you *can* do this!**

From now on, your beliefs are your springboard

That limiting belief is now gone. In its place stands a life-affirming replacement which will have a significant impact on how you feel about yourself and ways you interact with others.

That's enough for now. I am well aware there were other limiting beliefs on your list that you are anxious to terminate. Be patient, one at a time is plenty. You are not Arnie. Give it a day or two before you return to your limiting beliefs list. Work through it in order of emotional resonance, particularly those you numbered 2 and 3.

It boils down to this. *Human beings are their beliefs.* If you believe you can do it, you can. If you don't believe you can do it, you can't. Rest assured, you will be right every time.

Our beliefs act either as a springboard to our dreams or a brick wall that there is no way around. The tougher a goal, the greater the degree of certainty needed.

One of the joys of my own life is that I am constantly being s-t-r-e-t-c-h-e-d. Like anyone else who finds themselves in new territory, I might fall flat on my face. At such moments, I go back to beliefs. Do I TRULY believe that I will accomplish what I set out to do? If I feel the faintest tinge of concern, I identify the negative belief behind the doubt, find a replacement and go through the exercise.

This is not a chore. I don't do it with a sigh of resignation and an, 'Oh well . . . I suppose . . . if I must.' I do this because it has worked more times than I can count. I do so because I am committed to *being all that I can.* I know you are too.

Session Summary

1. Human beings create their own reality. Creating yours is the most important thing you will ever do, so get started.
2. Are you an elephant? What chains of belief do you need to break?
3. Make a list of your productive beliefs. Refresh that list every six months (more often if possible).
4. Go through your limiting beliefs and work on the top three as follows:
 i) Isolate your disempowering belief.
 ii) Construct an empowering replacement.
 iii) Recall three occasions when that replacement belief was true.
 iv) Run your film.
 v) Step into the screen.
 vi) Test your new empowering statement.

SESSION 5
The Voice of Doom

At this stage in the life-coaching cycle, one issue crops up time and again. Although thrilled at dumping beliefs that have held them back for so long, there is still an itch that many clients can't seem to scratch. 'This probably won't make much sense,' they say, 'but for some strange reason, I've started to feel uneasy.' I smile and reassure them that it makes perfect sense to me.

You may recall that the last session contained the following sentence: 'Our lives are determined by what we tell ourselves to be true.' **But have you ever wondered who is doing the telling and to whom?** Who, exactly, *is* that in my head? How did that thing get there? And would it please mind going away?

This session is about those conversations. Everyone really does have voices in their head. Yes, including you. Contrary to myth, this is not a sign of madness – not unless it's the voice of Mickey Mouse.

These conversations become particularly apparent at this point for a reason. Having dumped beliefs that no longer work (and probably never did), you find yourself on unfamiliar territory. This territory is energising, it is thrilling, you are finally ready to soar. However, it is also new – and new can be a bit worrying.

Disquiet is part of our human baggage. It is like a

worm that sneaks through a tiny porthole in our psyches, moving so slowly that we don't even notice it's there. Leaving an oily trail in its wake, the worm sneaks forward until it can be ignored no longer. I know it's arrived when clients scratch their heads, shuffle in their seats and tell me they 'don't know how to say this'. What has crept up on them is doubt.

Doubt is one of the manifestations of fear. You have dared to take on, and have now overcome, some of your biggest, most enduring demons. Compared to them, doubt is one of the small fry. Like all minnows, it takes care not to be seen. It is sneaky, subtle and sly. Some of things it will whisper in your ear include:

'This is never going to work.'
'Who on earth do you think you are?'
'Are you really sure about this?'
'It all sounds a bit weird.'
'You're out of your depth.'
'Come on, this is *you* we're talking about.'

I think of these voices that go round our head as being like Gollum's endless muttering in *The Lord of the Rings*. They are elusive and clever and slippery. They are constantly pretending to be on your side, offering an endless stream of 'helpful advice'. In fact they are simply making life harder by secretly undermining everything that you do. I suspect J.R.R. Tolkien might have based Gollum on a few voices of his own.

Your inner child is also part of the problem.

Psychotherapists ascribe many of our doubts to leftover scars from childhood. Lacking the confidence, understanding or love to recover from setbacks, the psychological development of the child remains incomplete. At times of challenge in later life, the inner child throws a wobbler and the adult is left – literally – holding the baby.

This session will teach you how to deal with your Gollum and your inner child. In the words of Friedrich Nietzsche: 'He who fights with monsters must take care lest he thereby become a monster.' The conversation in our heads must be brought to heel.

From time to time, some of those voices are useful. The healthier ones cajole you to get up in the morning, eat fruit with your Corn Flakes, brush your teeth, get out of the door, work hard, get on with your colleagues, come home in time to put your kids to bed and not to stay up half the night watching movies. These are different from your Gollum and inner child because they are rooted in conscience – occasionally irritating but basically doing a good job.

We've already discussed the flip side of this coin. Have you ever told yourself that nothing will ever work out, nobody will like you, you will never be happy, life will always be hard – and then you'll die?

How do these voices serve you? Could it be time to curtail their influence? **Could it be time to *stop listening*?**

Do not blame yourself, please. You have listened until now because you didn't know what else to do. You had no idea how to turn the damn things down!

The great news is that these voices in your head have an off button.

Take charge of your voices

> 'It isn't what you have, or where you are or what you are doing, that makes you happy or unhappy. It is what you think about.'
>
> DALE CARNEGIE

Let's start by putting a face to the voice. Who is it that's actually speaking? You *think* it's you. After all it *sounds* like your voice. But would you really be so relentlessly hard on yourself? Would you really talk to yourself in that abrupt, peremptory, my-God-you're-such-an-idiot manner?

Think for a moment. How did you learn how to do that? Who did you learn that *from*? The vast majority of the voices we hear in our heads are **parental.** These are the voices of one or other of our parents talking to us as if we were not yet ten.

Before I am accused of kick-starting a war between the generations, let me stress that it isn't strictly their fault. Your parents learned how to do it from their parents who learned how to do it from your grandparents . . . You get the picture.

Let me demonstrate how this works in practice. Before deciding to treat yourself to this book, some readers might have noticed a row going on in their head:

'What on earth do you need that for?'
'Actually, it looks good.'
'Haven't you got enough books already?'
'But it might help me.'
'Put it back, you know you'll never read it.'
'Oh be quiet, I'm buying it anyway.'

It's like one of those scenes from a pantomime. 'Oh yes, he did' / 'Oh no, he didn't.' A debate is going on which you don't want to hear, didn't ask for in the first place and always ends with one side or the other stomping off in a huff.

Think of a real example, one when you were giving yourself a hard time. You shouldn't have to look very far; most people 'beat themselves up' several times per day. Listen to it now. *Listen really carefully.* Go beneath the words and listen *to the tone, to the combination of words being used.* Whose voice is that really? Who do you hear?

Clients taken through this process usually turn to me with a look of utter disbelief. If it isn't Mum or Dad (which it will be 95% of the time), the voice is an echo of a particularly severe teacher or other authority figure entrusted with childhood discipline. *And they are still telling you what to do!* It's time to get rid of them once and for all:

- Go back inside and hear the voice once again. It should be less disconcerting now you know it's not yours.
- *Where* is the voice? Gently begin to check out the precise location.

- Is it in your head? If so, is it on the left side, the right side or bang in the centre? Be as exact as you can.
- It may be located in your chest (the classic storage area for stressful debris). It is often found inside the ear.
- Got it? OK. **Now add a face to the voice.** This part is easy because you already know whose face it is *BUT – we're going to change it.*

GIVING THE VOICE A MAKEOVER

- **I want you to add a beard to the face.** Exactly! Laughing at the image drains away all the power it uses to manipulate your emotional state. Feel yourself starting to relax, notice the tension begin to subside. The key to silencing the negative voice in your head is this – *gremlins hate being laughed at*. In the face of derision, their hold is released.
- **Now add a pair of NHS glasses or a curly red wig.** Put it in a skirt or a kilt, some spats or Spandex. Dress it as a nun or a clown or a baby.
- The next step always produces a smile. **Who is your favourite comedian?** Is it Victoria Wood, Steve Martin, Peter Kay, Woody Allen? When I am using this process, I usually go for Jim Carrey or Tommy Cooper. I only have to think of Cooper with that stupid fez on his head and the job is half done. Who is it for you? **Picture your favourite comic, see them** if you can but – this is much more important – *hear the sound of their voice.*

- When you are ready, summon back the voice of negativity, let it rant for a few moments, **then replace it with that of your comedian.** In a few seconds, it's gone. Rather than face further ridicule, your gremlin has packed its bags, upped and left.

This technique is stunningly effective. Practise it three or four times and you will be able to complete the entire process in 10–15 seconds.

No one gets rid of their negative voices entirely. As I suggested earlier, doubt is part of the human condition. You are (or so the rumour goes) human so doubt will creep back from time to time. However, specific gremlins do not return. Once you have banished a voice banging on about some particular irritation, it will be flushed out for good.

The voices in our heads are a habit. We fall into the habit of listening to them, considering their arguments and even following their advice. Use this exercise on a regular basis and you will find they appear less and less.

Expelling the voices of negativity has one other benefit too. Without all that din in your head, you may find not a lot is going on – it's called peace of mind. You may even find you enjoy it.

THIS IS WHY YOU CAN'T SLEEP

I mentioned earlier in the book that I work with insomniacs. You can always tell an insomniac. They are the ones who either look like they exist on a diet of Prozac or bounce into the room like the Duracell Bunny.

Many insomniacs are in denial about their condition. Once they've finished telling me how wonderful it is to need only three hours sleep per night because you get so much more done and how amazing the History Channel is at 4 a.m., we get down to solving the problem.

The problem is that their minds are overactive – whirling dervishes of schemes, ideas, conversations, plans, disappointments, frustrations, grudges and regrets. The middle of the night is not the time for such thoughts. Like our gremlins they have to be dealt with.

Three simple strategies invariably make a substantial difference to the sleep patterns of insomniacs (and thus their quality of life).

Sleep-solver step 1: Remove that notebook from the side of your bed. We covered that one in Session 1.

Sleep-solver step 2: The urge to get out of bed is driven by the idea that you have something far better to do than laze around sleeping. In fact, you've got a dozen better things to do, so let's make a start now. Run that one by me again . . . ? Human beings can exist without work but without sleep, we die. You need to sleep. You want to sleep. Here's how you will.

If sleep won't come and you must get of bed, **do something tedious.** I want you to think of the most boring tasks you can possibly envisage. The activities that are absolutely, positively, do-I-really-have-to, the last thing you would wish to get on with given half a chance – **which you do not have.** These might include:

polishing the silver
alphabetising your CDs
writing to Cousin June in Wisconsin
putting up the draught excluder
reading the collected works of Dostoevsky (forgive me,
    Fyodor, but they are a tad dull)

It's now the middle of the night. You can't sleep and decide to get up. **The aforementioned jobs – or worse – are the only things you are allowed to do.** Under no circumstances may you do some work, watch TV, go for a run, read a book etc., etc. You are not permitted to do anything useful or fun or (even minimally) interesting. Forget it.

I have found this approach generates instant results. Once the subconscious learns that rousing its poor victim (i.e. you) from bed will lead to hours of gut-wrenching boredom, then sleep becomes a far preferable option.

Sleep-solver step 3: This is an extension of the technique in the first part of this session. Hard-core insomniacs should nail 1 and 2 above first. Those who are simply looking to get back to sleep when they wake up can fast-forward to this one – and then start to s-l-o-o-o-w things down.

I was recently working with a golfer who was building a new house. One of the golden rules on the Professional tour is, if you want to lose your game in a hurry, call in the builders. Before you know it, all thoughts of triumph, trophies and glory will be displaced by nightmares about subsidence, cement and men in hard hats. Sure enough, that was what happened here. All night long, she was haunted by spectres of site meetings, work-shy bricklayers and budgets soaring through the roof. The price she paid was a howling case of the yips, a nervous affliction that is lethal for golfers. And, of course, she was getting no sleep into the bargain.

I cured her yips by alleviating the stress exacerbated by the building work. The key to restoring my client's sleep patterns was to silence the panic-stricken voices racing round her head during the wee hours.

In addition to putting a face to the voice (as above), there is one other technique that works wonders. In the days of vinyl records (CDs just aren't the same – plastic boxes, sleeve notes you can only read with a microscope), our grandparents owned discs that played at 78 rpm. I am not old enough to ever have bought one (honest!) but the house I lived in as a child had an enormous attic where my parents kept their dusty old records (Nelson Eddy and Jeanette McDonald held sway).

I brought a few down one day and tried to play them on my Dansette. The trouble was my record player didn't have a 78 rpm setting. When I tried to play those records at 45 rpm, all I got was what sounded like an extremely deep voice talking very s-l-o-o-o-w-l-y. A bit like Darth Vadar but slower and lower.

As we were sitting in her lounge, I asked my golfer to 'hear' the voices that were keeping her up. Once they were clearly audible, her task was to s-l-o-o-o-o-w the voices down until every word became a l-o-o-o-o-n-g, s-l-o-o-o-o-w, l-o-o-o-o-w drawl. She almost fell asleep doing the exercise.

Within days, her former sleep pattern had returned. More importantly, she stopped snapping at her partner, regained her sense of humour and realised that the house *would* get built whether she stressed about it or not.

It's time to stop listening

This is the shortest chapter in the book. Do not confuse brevity with degree of importance. Helping to silence their negative voices is one of the most enduring contributions that I make to the lives of my clients. These voices are devious. Until this session, you probably didn't realise they existed. Even if you did, you assumed it was **you** talking all along. *Oh, come on*. Are you really *that* bossy or bolshy or aggrieved or hectoring? *All the time?*

Make a point of practising with the tools in this session. I promise you'll be glad that you did.

Session Summary

1. The voices in your head have an off button.
   Learn how to use it:
   a) Where is the voice?
   b) Add a face.
   c) Give it a beard/dress/funny hat.

d) Change the voice to that of your favourite comedian.
2. If you can't sleep:
a) Do something tedious.
b) S-l-o-o-o-w right down – 78 rpm.

SESSION 6
Life Skills

Coaching, for me, is not just about tools. Transformation can undoubtedly be achieved through the skilful practice and successful absorption of the techniques I've described in the book thus far. However, it is my (not so humble) view that another dimension is also required. In the long term, I believe, the ability to change your life demands more than tools. I believe it also demands fresh ideas and attitudes. It is the readiness to acquire fresh knowledge and open the mind to new thoughts that makes the tools work. **Enduring transformation requires the acquisition of wisdom.**

Some of my sessions take several hours. The processes we go through involve the expenditure of a great deal of energy (by client and coach) and the results we achieve often go beyond expectation (again, on both sides). Over the years, however, I've had to own up to an uncomfortable truth. The key to change – what unlocks the door – is rarely what I *do*. Time after time, it is a word or a thought or a new perspective that drags clients out of the emotional quicksand.

This session is a collection of those thoughts, an illustration of the sudden perceptions that are 'the difference that makes the difference' and transform coaching sessions into something magical. Included here are ideas that clients have found helpful on such diverse subjects as love, God and creativity. For good measure, I have also included the single most powerful technique that I use.

Please don't try and absorb all this material in one sitting. Psychological indigestion is not a pretty sight. I recommend that you read through the session and extract one idea to begin with. Start with the concept you feel might resolve a current issue or anxiety and move on from there.

This, for me, is one of the most exciting of the sessions in this book. Admittedly, I am biased because I have seen these ideas in action and know what they can do. Transformational moments are not like slabs of concrete that drop from the sky and smack you on the skull. Those that leave the deepest impression are quiet, gentle and often tender. I hope you find these thoughts as powerful as those whose lives they've been instrumental in 'moving on'.

What's the worst that could happen?

Arjen Robben is one of the most gifted footballers in Europe. Shortly before joining Chelsea, in 2004, from PSV Eindhoven in Holland, he was diagnosed with testicular cancer. Fortunately, the condition was successfully treated and Robben was given the all clear.

However, Arjen Robben still bears the psychological scars of his illness. He can no longer bear even to read about anyone suffering from cancer. The terror of *what might yet happen* lives on in his mind. Robben is in the grip of a Catastrophic Fantasy. It is a syndrome to which we have all succumbed.

Imagine you've just started a new relationship. Your partner is gorgeous, sexy, funny and loving. You think he might be the one but your previous relationship ended in disaster. Although it's the last thing you want to happen, you imagine him telling you it just isn't working. You see yourself pleading with him to change his mind and feel your heart breaking all over again.

I went to prenatal classes before we had our first child. While everyone else there seemed to be a 'new man', I was a dinosaur. The other fathers-to-be couldn't wait to change nappies and get out of bed at 4 a.m. to rock baby to sleep. I had already declared my intention of moving out until the baby was six.

There were five prenatal classes in all and I turned up to four (a preview screening of *Pulp Fiction* was just too tempting). Anyway, at one session the midwife issued a warning:

'Under no conditions,' she roared, 'should you prod your baby in the middle of the night to make sure they are still breathing.'

Apparently, this is 'normal' behaviour for first-time parents. They are so fearful that their child might never wake up that, despite having spent hours getting the little darling to sleep, they wake junior up with a dig in the ribs.

How many Catastrophic Fantasies do you have every day? How often do you imagine the worst thing that could happen and switch straight to a movie of that event in your mind? Catastrophic Fantasies are incredibly enticing. They are like a motorway pile-up: you know you shouldn't gawp but can't help slowing down all the same. Catastrophic Fantasies are so tempting because everything revolves around *you*. You are the 'star' at the centre of the action, your suffering is unbearably intense and the script pans out in precisely the way you've predicted. You visualise the scene as if it was really happening and feel the emotions so strongly that they stay with you when the Director has called 'Cut!'.

And therein lies the danger. Catastrophic Fantasies would be harmless if they weren't so plausible. It is their proximity to experience that gives them their power. The problem is that fantasies become so believable that the distress they cause is real.

A lot of my clients suffer from Catastrophic Fantasies. They torment themselves about any number of events – fire, prison, bankruptcy, homelessness – that not only may never happen but have precious little chance of doing so. Some superstitiously maintain that 'dreaming them' limits the chance of these events actually taking place. Unless you enjoy the suffering that is caused by Catastrophic Fantasies, I suggest you do something to stop them.

Dealing with Catastrophic Fantasies

There are three phases to this job of taking charge of your Catastrophic Fantasies once and for all.

1. CONDUCT A REALITY CHECK

Catastrophic Fantasies are a bad habit. All habits are underpinned by patterns, and breaking the sequence stops the habit.

- Each time you emerge from a Catastrophic Fantasy, ask yourself this question: 'What is the likelihood of that event taking place?'
- Give it a number out of 100.

In the cold light of day, most Catastrophic Fantasies are ludicrous. When I ask clients to give them a number, most usually come up with 1–5%. A Catastrophic Fantasy that has, at most, a one-in-twenty likelihood of coming true really isn't very catastrophic at all.

Rating your Catastrophic Fantasies flips your relationship with them on its head. Instead of remaining in thrall to their power, you set the agenda. You have them when you want to but understand that they are, and always were, *an indulgence*. And if you choose not to have them, you won't.

2. USE THAT CATASTROPHIC FANTASY TO DO SOME GOOD

Once we have drained them of impact, Catastrophic Fantasies provide a fantastic opportunity. Damaged individuals are often their own saboteurs. At the point of achievement or realisation of their dreams, 'something' always seems to happen. Instead of stepping right over the chasm that's opened up, they peer over the edge and then pull back. However much they long to 'fly', it just never seems to happen. While external forces may sometimes be to blame, you can't kid yourself forever. If this is a syndrome that has blighted your entire life – as it has for many, many people – you may need to look in the mirror.

Part of the cause is your internal saboteur. It is a part of your psyche that feels uneasy with success. Until it is dealt with, any breakthroughs may prove elusive. If this is true in your case, please deal with it now. If you were sitting in my surgery, embarking on the following six-step journey is what we would do next.

Step 1. I would ask you to close your eyes and search for your saboteur. **We would take as long as it takes** – anything from 2 to 20 minutes.

Go inside and start searching. Don't try too hard, let your instincts take you in any direction they wish. Breathe *deeply* – inhaling through the nose and out through your mouth. You may need to wander around in there for a while until images begin to appear. Don't rush or judge these images, let them form in their own time, let them be what they are.

Step 2. What does your saboteur look like? I've already dropped a very broad hint. Your saboteur is familiar.

It is someone you know well. It is someone you know an awful lot about.

I am not going to reveal your saboteur's identity. Not now, anyway. This exercise is much, much more effective if you take the time to find out for yourself. What I will do – and I am trusting you not to peek – is provide the answer that applies to most people at the end of this chapter.

Step 3. When you can clearly see your saboteur, ask what it needs.

Being deprived of this was what forced the saboteur to stand in your way. Answers are likely to include love, support, information, strength or understanding. Can you provide what it needs?

Step 4. Clients often say that much as they would like to, they *cannot* provide (or bring themselves to provide) what the saboteur wants.

Try a different tack. Ask yourself **how** you can provide what it needs. There *is* a way, even if both of you have to compromise.

Step 5. Go on then, provide it. Interact with your saboteur until you both feel settled with the new status quo.

Step 6. Once the saboteur is at peace, **reclaim your own power.**

You will discover the saboteur *never wanted the power in the first place*. What it did want was listed in the answer to step 3. It was not having it that forced the saboteur to attract your attention in some other way. *Taking back this power will enable you to step right over the precipice and soar.*

Placating your saboteur is a profound piece of work. You will need to clear your head once it is done. Go for a walk or have a bath. Feel the power returning.

3. NEVER EVER, UNDER ANY CIRCUMSTANCES, GIVE YOUR POWER AWAY AGAIN
I want you to make a list of the times when you have given your power away in the past. This also takes as long as it takes.

- When do you hand over your power?
- Who do you give it to?
- How do you give it away?

Examples may include:

- Wives allowing their husbands to drag them to the pub every Saturday night.
- Husbands allowing their wives to arrange dinner parties with couples they cannot abide.
- Managers taking decisions that turned out to be damaging at the insistence of stronger-minded colleagues.
- Staff accepting the blame for errors that were not of their making.

When have you given your power away? Please do this exercise now.

★

★

★

★

★

★

★

The list should make you wince. Everyone you have given your power away to has prospered at your expense. Generosity is to be applauded, but some things should never be given away. Your power is one of them. I hope you feel disappointed. I hope you feel frustrated. I hope you feel *resolved*. Never, under any circumstances, will you give your power away again.

Keep those demons at bay

One last thing about psychological demons: they have a sneaky habit of creeping back and of morphing into new forms. Unfortunately, even once you've blitzed your saboteur, other enemies may lie in wait but psychological weapons will keep them at bay. You have already used your imagination superbly. Now I want you to use it to summon up a force that will protect you from further self-sabotage.

I want you to construct your own Private Internal Army. You are its Commander in Chief and can hand-pick whoever you like to marshal the troops. The objective of this army will be to provide you with protection and guidance. Don't worry; you don't have to be of military stock. My own pacifist views were perfectly summed up by Woody Allen in his movie *Love and Death*. 'In the event of war,' said Woody, 'I'm a hostage.'

I have my own army consisting entirely of hairy-chested, kilt-wearing, war-painted Scots (guess who's been watching too much *Braveheart*?). When I am faced with an issue in my life, I call a meeting of my Senior Officers. Not all are warriors. Some of my Generals are more renowned for their tactical acumen or logical prowess. My Officer Corps includes legendary figures from the worlds of music, politics and sport. All are drawn from crack units who have sworn absolute loyalty to their Commander in Chief. I know I can rely on their courage, discipline and devotion to duty.

However artificial the concept may appear on the page, I urge you to form your own army. Recruit whoever you want into your Officer Corps, develop a relationship with your troops. They need to trust you and you need to trust them. You will find their advice is clear and robust *and I advise you to take it*. If the cynic in you is insisting you will do no such thing, and this is the most ridiculous idea you've ever encountered, rest assured that all you are doing is accessing creative resources that have probably lain dormant for years.

Next time you find yourself under siege, call up your

troops. Saboteurs and demons get very short shrift from me. 'Oh yeah?' I mock. 'You and whose army?'

Message of love

One of the greatest conundrums we all face is how to find love. So much of our lives is spent searching for romance, and with a lack of success that is truly spectacular – irrespective of background, wealth or education. All that energy, all that time. Not to mention all that expense!

Suffering singles, miserable marrieds, gloom-laden gays – the search for love is a constant thread that runs through my work. This is a subject that could clearly fill a whole book – make that book*store* – but the couple of observations that follow provide a head start.

THE FREEWAY OF TRUE LOVE
Leonard Cohen is one of my favourite people. A singer/songwriter with a wholly undeserved reputation for 'miserabilism', the Canadian sage was featured in a documentary screened at some unholy hour on Sky TV.

Cohen had recently emerged from almost a decade in a monastery. Aware of his reputation as a ladies' man, the interviewer (who clearly had a crush on Cohen) asked what life had taught him about love. In his trademark husky tone, and with a trace of a smile on his lips, Cohen replied, 'The best definition of love I ever heard is this – **you go your way and I'll go your way too.**'

I don't remember anything else about the programme

– the songs that Cohen performed or any other questions he may have been asked. Those ten words were burned on my mind – **'you go your way and I'll go your way too.'**

Cohen's definition was everything I'd spent years attempting to condense. Love is freedom. Love is liberating your partner to lead the life that will enable them to be all they can possibly be. This is the life which, if you truly love them, you would wish them to have for themselves. If you love somebody, set them free.

Love is NOT need. Love is NOT constraint. Love is NOT COMPROMISE. Love is NOT a bargain – (e.g.) 'if you love me, I'll love you back.' Love is not shoehorning your partner into the 'right' clothes, the 'right' job or the 'right' life.

By the way, this applies equally to both sexes. In order to have and to hold, men and women need to stop worrying that their partners will leave or stop loving or outgrow them. In order to have love, you must be prepared to let go. If you cannot let go, what you have is not love but need: your love is not about your lover, it is about you.

I realise this is scary. The first reaction I often get is 'Without setting limitations, how do I know my partner won't leave?' It's a telling question. The inference seems to be that only limitations are holding the relationship in place.

Trying to change, or mould, other people is relationship poison. The way to avoid limitations but retain your perfect partner is to stand in True Self – which you should now be doing. True Self individuals *do* impose limitations – *on themselves*. They know what they will tolerate and what they will not. They know what kind of people to surround themselves with (i.e. those who will nurture their quest for self-definition) and which to avoid. They understand how to bring the best out of themselves and are committed to providing the same service for others.

Telling your partner what to do runs totally contrary to True Self behaviour. It you stand in True Self, you do not impose limitations because it puts your partner in *False Self*. You know it won't work. Very few people ever find their soul mates; and, as so few stand in True Self, that is hardly surprising. Their life is a lie and their partner is part of the fabric of their falsehood. You have a rare opportunity. Now that you stand in True Self, what would you want from your soul mate if they were standing before you? And what are you prepared to give them in return?

STRONG SINGLES = STRONG COUPLES
The singles circuit is full of people claiming they are 'ready' for marriage. Maybe they are, maybe they're not. But how do they know? What they actually mean by 'I'm ready' is either:

a) I'm listening to my instincts
b) I'm so desperate I'll take the first thing that comes along.

a) is clearly more helpful than b) but neither is actually much use.

There are crystal-clear differences between relationships that do and don't work. In my long and excruciating experience (I witnessed over two hundred divorces in my days at the Bar), one distinction outshines all the rest.

Both partners in a great relationship are perfectly fine on their own – and they were before they got together. Contented singles make a conscious choice to enter a new relationship which they then do not remain in through fear or need. The decision to stay or go is driven by the degree of ongoing happiness.

On the other hand, *poor relationships are often initiated by people sharing mutual terrors*. They were miserable by themselves and being together is the lesser of two evils. No matter how abusive or mutually contemptuous their relationship may become, the glue of dependency holds them together.

Many people who enter therapy or employ a life coach find romance soon afterwards. This is not one of those 'bizarre' coincidences, it happens time and again. Instead of attracting others with similar voids, clearing your path of psychological debris creates the foundation of the solid independence that leads to love. Miserable singles make miserable partners. Those who were fine on their own will be fine as a couple. It's up to you.

Silence is golden

'Silence is God's one and only voice.'
HERMANN MELVILLE

One of my favourite things in the entire world is writing scripts for cartoons. My brother is an extremely gifted artist and our work has appeared in newspapers and various other assorted publications. Roger and I have created strips about City traders, aesthetic aliens and a scheming computer called 'Chip'. My favourite is *Bananas*, a comic book about a bunch of gorillas at large in a safari park.

Trying to write jokes at my desk was always a waste of time. Scientists recently discovered that far more good ideas are unearthed in the bath than at work. Archimedes could have told them that for nothing. I find inspiration in the unlikeliest places: the car, the video shop – sometimes, the dry cleaners. Best, by far, has always been the train. If I ever get stuck, I grab a notebook and go for a ride on the London Underground. It works every time (when the trains are running, that is).

Partly through my connections at the BBC, I work with a lot of creative people who become blocked from time to time. What they need to know is how to regain inspiration – and fast. They've tried working longer and they've tried working harder but this only seems to make matters worse. Such an approach brings to mind the classic definition of despair – repeating the same thing time and again but hoping for a different result. What applies to creative souls in search of inspiration applies to everyone who needs to solve a problem in a hurry.

Back to childhood again. How many times were you and I lectured on the virtues of trying? And if that didn't work, all you had to do was try harder. *Why weren't we taught to do something different?* This is where my work begins. The road to recovery from any setback demands breaking the pattern. I'll sit down with the client and examine their pattern. We'll take it apart and create something that gets the job done.

Somewhere near the top of the list of patterns that need breaking is our fixation with thought. I realise what a shock this is – clients invariably struggle to take this one in – but *thinking doesn't work*. No matter what the problem, thinking is almost always the least effective way to fix it.

By 'thinking', I mean sitting at a desk, chewing a pencil and having a mull. I'm not saying it won't work *eventually*. What I am saying is it's incredibly slow and unproductive. Silence is much more effective.

Locating errant objects is a perfect illustration of how useless thinking can be. I've lost count of the number of keys I've helped people find. Next time you lose something, stop trying to work out where it is. Stop thinking about it over and over again in your mind. *That is not how the brain functions.* Locating missing objects demands a visual strategy.

The first step – as it so often is – is to sit still and *breathe*! Once you are completely calm, answer this question – *where did you last see the object gone missing?* Don't think about it, **see it.** Wherever you last saw your keys or credit cards, that is where they will be. Ignore the chatter in your head telling you this will never work. *Where did you see it?*

I've done this dozens of times on the phone. Pens,

books, mobile phones, cash, cheque books and enough jewellery to fill Hatton Garden – I've helped to find all these and more.

Franz Kafka said that if you sit still for long enough, the whole world will come to you. Dr Thomas Farewell – the eminent psychotherapist I mentioned in the introduction – spent six months, after being demobbed at the end of World War II, just sitting. This was, literally, he told me, just sitting within silence waiting for whatever he was meant to do with his life to reveal itself, which it did. It was trust in silence that led him to a career in medicine.

Circumnavigating London Underground's Circle Line was a great way to write jokes because my mind went quiet. Instead of fretting about a blank page or deadlines, my mind would wander off. I'd stare with incredulity at the antics of other commuters (why **do** people smell their ear wax?) or check out posters offering cheap phone deals (I know ten ways to phone India for 8p). In the space between musings – when I wasn't 'trying' – jokes would appear.

HOW TO GO QUIET ON CUE

Meditation is a great place to start the search for silence. It took me years to get around to learning meditation – I thought you'd have to sit cross-legged on the floor (doh!) – but have found it a constant source of peace and sustenance for over twelve years. And there's absolutely no humming.

Meditation is a chance to stop doing and 'be'. Thoughts go round your mind in the same way as normal but, instead of reacting, responding and preparing to 'do', the meditator just observes. Meditation slows the mind down and this creates the space for something new to appear.

Meditation takes many forms. Cooking, gardening and playing a musical instrument all have hugely meditative properties provided you are totally absorbed in the experience. Absorption is all. Stop *thinking*. A dog helps. A fortnight before starting this book, after years of incessant nagging from my children, we bought a puppy. Taking the dog for walks has proved a wonderful way of gathering ideas through silence. Her constant yapping while I'm eating my lunch is not quite so useful.

FINDING THE SOURCE OF YOUR INSPIRATION
There is a structure to the process of creation from silence, one that many clients have found helpful. Martin Perry and I developed this template for golfers but the method is equally effective for writers, inventors and teachers.

- Create a space inside – use awareness of your breathing to quieten thought.
- Take in and appreciate your environment. If you are outside, notice (but softly) the sunlight, flowers, grass, temperature, barometric pressure or wind. If you are sitting inside, listen for the sounds of the heating or the traffic, and look afresh at any paintings, possessions or decorations. Find images that will inspire and relax.
- Trust. Resist all temptation to try.

- Retain a sense of the outcome you want to achieve. Feel what it will be like when you have done so.
- Surrender. Thinking is not, never was and never will be, a match for acquiescence.

Some of the Beatles' greatest songs emerged in precisely this fashion. 'Nowhere Man' is a John Lennon classic that he wrote at 4 a.m. He had been up all night 'trying' to compose something for the *Rubber Soul* album. It was when on the point of giving up and going to bed that Lennon 'surrendered' and the melody arrived. He later recalled that he let his mind go and the song just appeared.

Paul McCartney had a similar experience with 'Yesterday'. McCartney described the track as arriving 'fully formed' when he was sitting at the piano. He simply wrote down the notes he could hear in his head. The experience was so mystical – McCartney was convinced he'd copied the song from the radio – that he took over a year to play his most famous track to the other Beatles. 'Is this by someone else or did I write it?' Paul reportedly asked.

No *more* deals

One of my own favourite songs is 'Running Up That Hill' by Kate Bush. Apart from the keening melody, what people remember about that track is one line that resonates across the generations: 'If I only could, I'd make a deal with God.'

How many people make deals with God in child-hood? 'I'll be really good if I get a bike for Christmas.' 'If I get top marks, I promise I'll never hit my brother again.' One friend of mine swears that Liverpool FC lost the FA Cup Final to Manchester United in 1977 because he didn't go to synagogue that morning. Man United's centre-forward had nothing to do with it.

If it's not God, it's our parents. 'I'll eat the peas but not the Brussels sprouts' (that was me), or, 'I'll wash the car if you give me a lift to the station.' Finally, we make deals with ourselves. 'One more pack and then I'll stop smoking.' 'One more cake and I'll get on the treadmill.'

Deals put boundaries around our potential. They inhibit, suffocate and imprison. Some of those deals will be made with the soundest of intentions. Others are just plain dumb. The worst kind of deals are those we make with our subconscious. And absolutely the worst of *those* deals is the kind that goes: 'If I have a good day today, I'll have a bad one tomorrow.'

One of the most common syndromes that I help people work through could be described as 'For Every Up, There's A Down'. Vast swathes of thoughtful, intel-ligent, mature individuals genuinely believe they are not 'allowed' to have two good days in a row.

I want to dig out the weed at the root of this false-hood – and, though it's not his fault, it all goes back to God. Poor God. Create a world in seven days and what do you get? – 100 million years of flak (and counting). Poverty, famine, war, disease, divorce, depri-vation – God gets the blame for all these and more.

The deals we make with ourselves are founded on a fundamental misconception. Good boys and girls go to heaven. Bad boys and girls go to hell. I can hear the howls of righteous indignation from here. *A fundamental misconception!* Who am I to suggest any such thing? This, after all, is a principal tenet of religious faith across the globe. 'Reward and Punishment' is one of the cornerstones of any decent, civilised society. How dare I dispute such a time-honoured dictum? How do I *know* it isn't true? Simple really. Just ask yourself this question. **Why would God need us to be good?**

Let me repeat that for those who cannot believe what they've just read: Why would God *need* us to be good? I'll go further, why would God need us to be or to do anything at all? Is God needy? That can't be right. God is all-powerful. So God must already have everything that he or she needs. Would God prefer us to be 'good'? That presumes God has preferences – which presumes God doesn't already know how things will turn out. That can't be right, either. So God has no preferences.

People are needy, not God. *People* have preferences, God doesn't. What are the implications of this argument? Just one, really. We are free. Free from fear, free from *the threat of retribution*. Free to be as much as we can. All dogmas are man made. People give them substance – people *choose* to give them substance – by cloaking their (*yes, their*) beliefs in divine 'authority'.

Ask yourself, what *could* God need? – power, popularity, obedience? For what purpose? I lived with such a 'God' for the first forty years in my life. A God who is angry, jealous, vengeful, judgemental, intolerant and has *no* sense of humour. This is the God with the draconian rulebook. The one that will not be argued with or disobeyed or talked to in 'that' tone. Oh, and he thinks that sex is disgusting.

At 42 years of age, I realised this did not make – and never had made – any sense. I remembered what I had always known. I did believe in God, I always had; just, not that one. The God I believe in is understanding, reasonable, rational, generous, funny, enabling, empowering and *present*.

Be honest. Have you suspected any of this all along but did not dare believe it for fear of the consequences (to your loved ones, your business, your health etc.)? Stop being afraid – *and be free*. If you are free, you do not make deals because there are no deals to be made! And, of course, there never were.

This understanding changed my life. I stopped bartering what I didn't have for something I might or might not get. For the first time, I truly understood that abundance is the natural order of the universe, that not only can you have everything you want but *you are meant to have it*.

Right here is one of the biggest distinctions between high achievers and the rest of humanity. *High achievers don't have a quota. They expect to win all the time and they do*. When money, love, fame etc. fall at their feet, they don't believe a price must be paid. They *Dare*. They dare to regard success as their birthright. They are RIGHT. *It is. And it is yours, too*. Please stop making deals. They are the act of an emotional four-year-old. Promising that 'I'll forfeit x if you'll give me y' is utterly and completely disempowering. What you gain is an illusion. What you lose is all too real.

The Black Box technique

Last but not least in this session, here is that best-ever technique that I promised you. The Black Box technique wipes out distractions. Distractions are:

- a colleague at work who can't stop blowing their nose.
- parents-in-law who make your skin itch when they come to stay.
- flashbulbs popping at the top of a professional golfer's backswing.
- minor irritations that assume gigantic proportions.

The Black Box technique obliterates them all. I'll explain how it worked in the case of a famous footballer, but the Black Box is equally effective at removing *any* distraction, sporting or otherwise.

A couple of years ago, I was invited to work with a Premiership football side that was heavily reliant on one of their strikers. The striker hadn't scored for eight games, the team had gone into freefall and the manager's job was on the line.

I wasn't exactly greeted with open arms. More like a leper. The fact I had been recommended by another Premiership manager cut no ice at all. When I walked into the canteen where the players were gathered, they immediately drifted to the other side of the room. In fact, they didn't so much drift as sprint.

The reluctance of UK sportsmen to work with sports psychologists is based on a fundamental misconception – they think I am a psychiatrist. They are terrified I will get them to hug their inner child or probe their relationship with their parents. Peer pressure is another issue. If you are seeing a 'sports psych', there must be something 'wrong' with you and you definitely do not want your team-mates to know what it is, let alone the *News of the World*.

The manager was smarter than I thought. After training, he brought ALL the forwards in to meet me. Not only did this avoid singling out the misfiring striker, but highlighted the fact that none of the others could hit a barn door. We talked for an hour about the team's lack of goals. Once the boss had left the room, the real truth emerged. The striker was not only the best player in the team but the most popular member of the entire squad. He was stuck on 99 career goals and everyone knew it. The entire team had become obsessed with the centre-forward hitting three figures. So obsessed that it had become a **distraction.**

That was the word I'd been waiting for. I promised – note, *promised* – everyone in the room that they need worry no longer. I asked the 99-goal striker (who was already feeling a lot better after hearing how much his team-mates cared) to stay behind and work with me for 10 minutes.

'You're going to fix me in 10 minutes?' he snickered.

'You'd better believe it,' I replied. I told him we would be using the Black Box technique.

The Black Box technique is – and I write this next sentence without the slightest hesitation – the most powerful sports-psychology tool in the world. It never fails. I have used it on well over a hundred occasions and **it has worked every single time.** The technique places the distraction in a 'safe' place within your subconscious. Securing it there provides the 'distract-ed' (e.g. the striker) with a pause, becalming the distraction itself. Reducing the distraction enables performance to return to previous levels. When the distraction re-appears (if it does so at all), it is far too late to do any damage.

I want you to learn the Black Box technique for yourself. The entire exercise, as I assured our centre-forward, takes 10 minutes at most. Think of something that preys on your nerves, read through the instructions and then find somewhere where you will not be disturbed.

WORKING WITH THE BLACK BOX

- Sit down, relax and close your eyes.
- Begin by taking a few deep breaths – allow the air in through your nose and out again through your mouth. Slowly.
- Imagine you are sitting in your favourite chair. You know what kind of chair it is: divan, couch, settee, rocking chair. Notice the material of the chair as you sit down, the colour and any pattern. Feel the

chair against your back and legs, allow yourself to be completely supported.

- As you look around, you realise that you are in a room looking out onto your favourite view. That scene may be a beach or a mountain range or a glorious countryside. Make it somewhere you love to be and know really well.
- Take in the view and stay with it for a few seconds.
- As you come back in to your inner room, you notice that in front of you is a desk. Choose a desk that you like. It may be one that you have used many times or a brand-new desk you have just designed. See it in as much detail as you can – is it made of wood or glass? Is it brown or black? Is it sturdy or light?
- On the desk you observe a sheet of paper and pen. Pick up the pen now. Feel the weight of the pen in your hand. *Feel that you are actually holding the pen.*
- Now – write your distraction on the sheet of paper (e.g. in the case of the striker, it was 'My 100th Goal'). Write as much or as little as you like. It might be one word or a couple of paragraphs. *See the words as they start to appear in your own handwriting.*
- Once you have finished, put down the pen and see what you have written. Now pick up the sheet of paper and fold it in half.
- As you turn around, you notice a Black Box behind you. The box is on the floor and has a slot for posting notes through.

- Take your note and post it through the slot in the Black Box.
- Turn back again and look out onto your favourite view. Enjoy those images for a few more seconds and open your eyes.

The immediate reaction of everyone I take through the Black Box exercise is that it's far too simple to work. And yet it does. Time and time *and time* again. Once you have completed the exercise, think about your distraction. How does it feel now? The answer I look for is a shrug. Not 'It's gone!' or 'I feel like a new person!' A shrug will do fine. That was the response I got from the striker. We shook hands and he left.

We met up again ten days later. By now, he was on top of the world. Not only had he scored his 100th goal but his 101st and 102nd, too. The team had secured back-to-back victories and the manager wanted me to work with the team's defence. 'We've got a big match against the local opposition coming up at the weekend,' he winked. 'Their crowd can be a bit of a distraction.' The striker had let the secret of the Black Box out of the bag. 'You win,' he smiled as we met in the canteen. 'One or two of the boys would like to have a word.'

BLACK BOX REVISITED

There is a second part to the Black Box exercise that takes precisely 10 seconds. Please do this once the distraction has subsided. *Do not ignore it under any circumstances*:

- Close your eyes and return to that favourite armchair looking out at that view.
- Turn around, open the lid of the Black Box and extract your sheet of paper.
- How do you feel when you read what is written? (Indifference is the usual response.)
- Turn back around and enjoy the view for a few more seconds.
- Open your eyes.

This second part of the exercise is critical. Without this reiteration, the distraction may creep back in and impair future performance. More importantly, *two items cannot go in the Black Box at once*. It must be emptied if you want to use it again.

The Black Box technique is not just for sportsmen. It will sweep away any number of irritants that have bugged you for far longer than you care to remember. Use it well.

Session Summary

Key thoughts from this session:

1. What was your last Catastrophic Fantasy?
   Did it pan out?
   What about the one before that?
   Do you really have to be so afraid?
2. Who was your saboteur?
   As I hope you discovered, in the vast majority of cases, your saboteur is you!

3. Stop giving your power away.
4. Do you love out of choice or need?
   Are you standing in True Self in your relationship?
5. Be inspired. Stop thinking!
6. Create a Black Box for your distractions.
   Don't forget, it must be emptied each time.

You Are *Lucky*

'Luck be a lady tonight' – it's a great moment in *Guys and Dolls*. Sky Masterson and the crapshooting crew are singing their plea to Lady Luck to smile on their dice. In doing so, they are exposing their belief that luck is capricious, fickle, whimsical and liable to desert them at any moment.

Most gamblers would agree. It was the slings and arrows of outrageous misfortune that led them to back that sluggish greyhound or horse with three legs in the first place. Luck is a cold-hearted shrew that has wrecked their finances, their relationships and lives. If only they had been *luckier*.

Luck, like God, has had a seriously bad press. Humanity has been obsessed about luck for hundreds of years but done surprisingly little to try and shift the odds in its favour. On reflection, that may not be entirely fair. I know several people who refuse to walk under ladders, who touch wood when things are going well and burst into 'that' song if they see a magpie.

In fact, superstition does nothing to shift the odds in your favour. It is, however, superbly effective at having the opposite impact. Here's why.

Each act of superstition sends a series of messages

to your subconscious. The messages go something like this:

1. We have a problem.
2. It's beyond my control.
3. I don't know what to do about it.
4. I'm feeling anxious.
5. I can't just sit here.
6. I've got to do something.
7. This doesn't make sense but I'm doing it anyway.
8. That was ridiculous.

Superstition might make the Bogey Man go away for a few moments, but the long-term damage is incalculable. Faced with a challenge that demands an adult response, the remedy chosen is one that *even the person concerned has good reason to suspect may be of no use whatsoever*. The challenge itself is perceived as too powerful. The individual imagines themselves as helpless in the face of overwhelming odds.

Behaviours of this kind are a virus. They are an easy option. They are not the act of a self-determining adult but the act of a victim. They supplant faith in the self with faith in something 'out there'. They don't 'work' (i.e. add power to a meaningful life) and they sap confidence in the conviction that anything else will work either. Superstition is the polar opposite of my definition of confidence – *superstition is a relationship of **mistrust** between 'you' and 'you'*. As you'll have gathered, I am not a great fan.

Luck doesn't happen by accident

From the earliest days of my coaching career, I noticed something strange. My clients appeared to get luckier. As I mentioned in Session 2, the first golfer I ever worked with won the very next tournament he played in. The odds of this happening were around 10:1. He won the next tournament too. The odds of both happening were nearer 10,000:1.

I absolutely, fundamentally, do not believe in co-incidence. This is a subject we'll explore in greater detail later in Session 9 but, for now, all I will say is that coincidences arouse my curiosity. Assuming for a moment that there *is* no such thing as a coincidence, what on earth was going on with my golfer?

I began to think about the ingredients of luck. Could there be a potpourri of ingredients that would improve my clients' chances of attracting the outcomes they desired? Could I brew up a magic recipe that would turn the odds in our favour? And, if so, how much is a one-way ticket to Las Vegas?

A warning, if I may. What follows will provide you with a series of clues (that's *clues*, not solutions) that may improve the degree of fortune you experience in future. This is not a secret formula to untold wealth and happiness (sorry about that). The contents of this chapter must be placed strictly in the context of the rest of the book. Anyone who just happens to be having a quick leaf through and stops at this point (Hi!), believing they are about to discover how to get lucky, should go back to the start like everyone else. I know, I'm no fun.

The conviction that you are lucky is well worth acquiring. It provides an intoxicating sense of personal affirmation and an unshakeable belief that any hurdle can be overcome. ***Luck is just too important to be left to chance.*** Serendipity needs the helping hand that we are about to provide.

Exercise your spirit of generosity

> 'A man there was, tho' some did count him mad,
> The more he cast away, the more he had.'
> JOHN BUNYAN (from *Pilgrim's Progress*)

Have you had enough of not having enough? *Really* had enough? Not just 'it would be quite nice to have more if I could' kind of enough? More 'I'm thoroughly sick of not having the things I know I could have if only I could sort myself out' type of enough?

Lucky people share a secret. They don't keep it a secret, it's not *meant* to be a secret but no one believes them when they explain what it is. So, as their un-official unappointed representative, here goes: **whatever you want, give it away.** Simple really.

If you want love, give love
If you want money, be charitable
If you want support, be supportive
If you want peace, be peaceful
If you want to be happy, make others laugh
If you want to win, relish the triumphs of others

See – you don't believe me either. Who do you know that you would consider – and would consider themselves – to be lucky? Go on, write down a few names. Three will do.

Are any of these lucky people . . .

Angry
Hostile
Inhospitable
Jealous
Mean-hearted
Mean-spirited
Miserly
Resentful

No, they emphatically are not. As the saying goes – what you give is what you get. Actually, I'd put it slightly differently. What you *are* is what you get.

Let's get the hippie speak out of the way. This is not, repeat not, about karma. I am uneasy with the whole concept of karma because, somewhere along the way, reward and punishment found their way into the mix: i.e. he who is vindictive shall receive vindictiveness in return. It's all a bit too biblical for me. The truth is one that needs no explanation . . . Smile at strangers and you get a smile back. Scowl at strangers and you get a scowl back. **What you are is what you get.**

Although I emerged from secondary school having failed my Physics O-level exam, even I can comprehend the scientific rationale involved here. In two sentences, it goes like this:

The universe is a huge field of electromagnetic energy. Energy, by its nature, is intended to flow.
Blockages run counter to this natural order.
(Sorry, that was three.)

Everything in our world is subject to exactly the same forces:

- Whatever is permitted to flow will expand.
- Whatever is blocked will contract.
- Hang on to love and you lose it.
- Hang onto your friends and you won't have them for long.
- Hang onto your kids and watch them squirm away from your grasp.

Money is the best example of all. Money is simply a form of energy – no easier or more difficult to attract than any other form. There is no great barrier to wealth. If you want to grow rich, stop thinking of money as (sharp intake of breath) *money*! As something you don't have and which is, therefore, a 'problem'. Wealth is not generated by hanging on to what you have. The Midas Touch is born of flow. A mindset of investment (in businesses, ideas, people) keeps the energy circulating. I can see the spendthrifts rubbing their hands in glee. Forget it. Wealth begins by working with what you have, not what you don't. Find your justification somewhere else.

Beliefs are part of the equation. Money is not, and

never was, the root of all evil. Money is not dirty or nasty or wrong – and there is nothing virtuous about poverty. This is something I have had to contend with, myself. Getting paid for helping people sort out their lives used to bother me greatly. I guess I wanted to be Father Theresa. It felt awkward to be reconnecting people with themselves and then asking them for a cheque. No wonder I was financially challenged.

Then I started working with sportsmen and women who were earning tens of thousands of pounds per week. They needed me because they weren't winning. After we worked together, they did win. I finally understood that what I did added value. Unless, and until, you value what you do – and charge what you are worth – why should anyone else? I stopped feeling guilty and the money appeared. What you *are* is what you get.

Try this for one week – just one week. Give away whatever you want to attract into your life. It will come soon enough, but avoid looking for an instantaneous return. Anxiety is a blockage – as is fear, pessimism, small-mindedness, restlessness and impatience. All such blockages will prohibit the arrival of whatever you seek; not because they are 'bad' or 'sinful', but because that kind of thinking just doesn't work. We live in an electromagnetic universe; these blockages inhibit the flow of its energy – and there is no way around the damage they cause.

What Kylie taught me . . .

In January 1988, I wrote a centre-page spread for the *Sunday People*. The article was about the rising wave of girlie pop stars – Tiffany and Belinda Carlisle were among them – and the paper added one of their own.

I had barely heard of Kylie Minogue. I was far too busy to watch *Neighbours* and much too hip to sully my ears with anything from the so-called 'Hit Factory' of Stock/Aitken/Waterman. I wasn't alone. None of the cooler publications I wrote for wanted anything to do with Kylie and I turned down several opportunities to meet the rising star from Down Under.

One afternoon, I was wasting time playing video games with one of my editors when the conversation turned to the Kylie phenomenon. Both of us had witnessed something that was totally unique. Writer after reluctant writer had been frog-marched in to interview Ms Minogue. Every single one of them fully intended to gain their revenge by slaughtering her in print. Not one could bring themselves to do so. This was not just clever PR. Something else was going on and I decided to find out what it was.

It was Kylie. The writers all reported the same thing. She was 'kind', 'generous' and 'a total sweetheart'. Kylie radiated a blend of qualities in the face of which hard-bitten cynicism could not be sustained. I suspected there were other factors at play. We all meet special people from time to time, but few generate such an improbable response.

It was some years later when I worked out what it was. Kylie had returned to prominence, riding a wave of popularity that had little to do with the quality of her music ('Spinning Around'? – come on, it was the hotpants). This time I got it. What you are is what you get. Yes, Kylie *was* kind and generous and a total sweetheart. More to the point, she gave these unsuspecting journalists a chance to be kind and generous and total sweethearts back. And they took it.

For all the attention surrounding her bum, Kylie Minogue's career is not about her beauty or her songs. People aren't stupid. They know (I love you, Kylie, but . . .) her voice is tinny, she's cute but hardly charismatic and her recorded output will be forgotten once she has disappeared from the spotlight. Kylie is adored because of what she sets off in *her audience*. Kindness, generosity and sweet-heartedness are not attitudes, these are states. It's not something you have, it's something you *are*. What Kylie gives people is a glimpse of something that is, or was, or still could be in them. Kylie is neither so impossibly beautiful nor so outrageously gifted that what she represents is beyond aspiration. Kylie could be you.

How do you know if you are lucky?

I'm serious. How do you *know* if you're lucky? Ask most people that question and the answer would generally be 'I just am,' or 'I just know I'm not.' That's not much use. Luck is a massive component of our sense of self-worth; yet, what I constantly hear is that deciding whether you are lucky or not boils down to some kind of 'I think so'.

One of the main causes of this uncertainty is looking outwards, not inwards. When it comes to luck, comparisons are invidious. As I explained in Session 2, one of the most damaging aspects of the human character is our obsession with comparing the quality of our lifestyles with those of other people.

I live in a very pleasant area of North London. Nothing posh, just pleasant. We have shops and parks and schools and a mainline railway station that goes straight to Waterloo. Personally, I am as happy as a pig in . . . er . . . mulch. I, clearly, am deluding myself. Whenever I get together with friends or neighbours in our area, they are always moaning about how much happier they would be if their house/flat was on the fringes of the leafy parkland, with its ponds and hills, that is Hampstead Heath or 'somewhere closer to town'.

Oh, would they? I know people who live 'on the Heath' and they seem to exist in perpetual fear of being burgled. I know people who live in town and would 'do anything' for a garden. The grass really is always greener – somewhere else.

Men and women are equally at fault. Advance warning – readers of both sexes are about to be grievously offended. Here goes:

Men are ambitious.

Women are competitive.

When you've finished scoffing at the behaviour of the other lot, we'll move on:

- The Alpha Male inside the modern hunter/gatherer is rarely more satisfied than when looking down his nostrils at lesser members of the tribe. In

business, romance and sport, men need to
out-achieve other men.

- Women are in competition with each other. If they
are not vying for boyfriends or assessing their
place on the pecking order of sexual attraction,
they are informing the world of the superior
quality of their clothes or holidays or the
attainments of their kids.

Older readers will remember a famous comedy sketch
from the sixties in which John Cleese, Ronnie Barker
and Ronnie Corbett played (respectively) members of
the upper, middle and lower classes. Although Corbett
(the lowest in the pecking order) was miserable, Cleese
and Barker were perfectly content; they knew that
what really mattered in life was having someone to
look down on. None of this would be of much conse-
quence but for one thing . . .

> Negative comparisons are one of the principal
> catalysts for feeling unlucky.

Focusing on the wealth, marriages or accomplishments
of other people puts a negative spin on your own. Unless
your name is Roman Abramovich, there is *always*
someone with more money than you. You – yes you!
– need to stop comparing yourself with anyone else.
So, back to my original question: how can you tell if
you are lucky?

STOP GUESSING, BE SURE

Reeves Weedon was born to teach. He happens to be one of the finest golf coaches in the world but could have taught anything. He works from dawn till dusk helping people discover the best in themselves. Reeves' lessons last one hour of which 15 minutes are used to hit little white balls while 45 minutes are spent chatting. It's the chat that turns his players into champions.

I love watching Reeves in action. Changing golf swings is an extremely fraught process, a sure-fire recipe for student protest. 'That feels terrible!' is one oft-repeated cry as balls fly towards the car park. 'I keep feeling that the ball will go left/right/sideways/backwards,' is another. After all these years, I know what's coming: '*What you feel may not be real*,' Reeves grins. He's right, too.

When clients tell me they feel blessed or cursed, I turn into Reeves. 'What you feel may not be real,' I parrot. We need to do better. We need to be certain.

SO, HOW LUCKY ARE YOU?

What do you measure – **about yourself** – that provides a meaningful indication of how lucky you are (or not)? You don't, huh? You didn't even know luck could be measured. Well, it can. But only by you, this is not a job for MORI. Time to get out your pen. Quit moaning, it's been ages since I asked you to do any work.

I want you to consider the quantifiable elements of your life. These are the areas in which your degree of fortune can be realistically assessed. My list would include:

You Are Lucky

Car	Intelligence
Childhood	Marriage
Communication	Money
Family	Musical ability
Friends	Peace
Health	Sex
Hobbies	Social Skills
Home	Sporting talent

Please draw up a list of your own. Your headings will almost certainly be very different from mine. Be certain to pick out the areas of your life that are really important to you.

Now, think carefully; this next bit is tricky. Place a tick or a cross beside each item on your list to indicate whether you feel lucky about it or not. Yes, I was kidding about tricky. Are you absolutely sure? Go back over the list one more time and make any adjustments in the light of fresh realisations.

OK, so what have you got? Are you better off than you thought (most people are, but will do anything before they'll admit it)? Or has the hand of fate smacked you in the teeth more often than you'd realised?

Divide the number of categories that made up your list by the number of ticks you gave yourself and turn that into a percentage. This is your Luck Baseline. For example, I marked 12 ticks beside my list of 16, producing a baseline percentage of 75%.

As the months go by and you put the lessons of this session into practice, I recommend that you return to this list and do another calculation. Not tomorrow;

give it a few weeks. Luck, I repeat, is far too important to be left to chance. Improving yours starts here.

Count your blessings

Most days pass by in a blur. Shortly before midnight, you slump exhausted (or drunk) in your chair, grateful just to have survived. Reviewing the activities of the day never crosses your mind. Getting through the damn thing in the first place was quite bad enough without dredging up the 'highlights' all over again. Anyway, what point would it serve? What good would it do? Far better to put it behind you, get off to bed and trust tomorrow will be marginally less awful. Sounds about right? Well done. Continue thinking that way for the next thirty years and you *will* die bitter, twisted and lonely. Enjoy.

One of the principal distinctions between people who lead lives that are either rich or desolate is **what they notice.** What tends to get the lion's share of attention are the trials, tribulations and reversals that are undoubtedly part of our daily existence. The good stuff hardly gets a look in. What about the high points, triumphs and pleasures that must be lurking in there somewhere?

> If you are not seeing the good stuff, all you are seeing is bad.

In order to be lucky, you've got to *feel lucky*. And you can't feel lucky without evidence. No matter how great the chip on your shoulder, there will be more than enough evidence that life is grand if you know where to look.

The following exercise is one I do every day. *And I mean every single day of my life.* I badger each and every one of my clients into doing it as well. Now it's your turn to be pestered. This exercise falls squarely into the 'It's so simple it can't possibly be any good' category. But when was complexity a reliable indicator of worth? Once it starts working for you, pass it on.

Give me a 'high five'

Before you go to bed each night, plug in the hard drive of your memory. Look back over the events of the day and register – you don't have to write them down – five good things that happened.

They do NOT have to be huge or magical or amazing. My own list from yesterday (when I caught a cold, the weather was shocking and my phone went phut) looked like this:

- I finished Session 6 of the book.
- A package I'd been waiting for arrived from Amazon – and nothing was missing.
- Steak and chips for dinner.
- A new till opened in Sainsbury's as I arrived at the crowded checkout and was preparing to seethe (I told you – I don't do queues).
- The puppy slept on my feet.

Small pleasures count too. Even on the worst days, there *will* be five moments worthy of inclusion. It could be the sun coming out (I live in England, so that is *always* worth celebrating), going for a walk, a smile from a stranger, a joke you've overheard, a drink with a mate or a space appearing in a crowded car park. Five should be no trouble at all. Get into the swing and a dozen is a doddle.

Repetition is the linchpin of this exercise. The first time you do it, enjoy the surprise of having had a better day than you remembered. By the second week, you will note a subtle lift in your general mood, prompted by the subconscious recognition that every day has much more than you thought worth celebrating.

Do not stop there. Within a month (and this is where the real fun starts), you will start to clock the pleasures of life **as they happen.** Now you get a double whammy – you feel great now *and* later on. Keep going for a few more weeks and you will have amassed a store of (at least) 200 positive events. The rest is automatic. Five positive occurrences each day – every day – is more than enough to convince any jury that 'I am lucky'. Even the most hardened pessimist will struggle to put together a convincing argument that their life is a drag.

Most of this chapter is filled with ideas on how to increase your share of good fortune (not that there is any 'share' to be had, good luck is infinite), **but you don't have to 'get' lucky; you already are.** This next exercise is all the proof you need.

Luck in business – *create your own good fortune*

Let me tell you how this book came about. One of my 10-year-old son's best friends is called David Lipowicz. David's dad, Simon, is a computer genius who is always coming round to fix my PC (every four minutes).

It was during one of those visits that Simon mentioned that his sister was married to an Argentinian sports agent called Julio who happened to be working for Mel Stein, a prominent sports agent who used to represent Paul 'Gazza' Gascoigne in his ace-footballer days. Simon suggested that Julio and I meet up for a drink. Julio went one better than that: he also invited Mel – who was not only curious about my work with Premiership footballers but also my background as a journalist. 'You should write a book,' said Mel. 'I'll give you the number of my agent.'

Mel put me in touch with David Riding at the MBA Literary Agency. We had a preliminary chat and, when *The Challenge* started its TV run, David was straight on the phone. 'If you'll write a chapter and an outline, I'll send it to some publishers,' he said.

Our timing was perfect. The chapter was warmly received by virtually all the publishers it went to and I eventually signed with the publishers Hodder & Stoughton. Our packed, 'get to know you' informal chat – it felt like half the department turned up – was all I needed to plight my proverbial troth.

What do you make of this story? Would you say that *Dare* was 'meant to be'? Was I just in the right place at the right time? *Do you think I was just lucky?*

When I quit the Bar, I applied for a job selling life insurance. As part of the interview, candidates were asked to go on to the street outside and get the names and addresses of ten passers-by. I thought it was a bit sleazy but pretended to be conducting research on behalf of the council. It took me eight minutes. Needless to say, they gave me the job and I was fast-tracked onto a training course that very afternoon.

Page 1 of the manual left little room for argument. 'Most insurance is sold through contacts,' it said. 'Think of everyone you know. Give them a call. Be prepared to contact their friends and families.' The supervisor waited for us to cast our eyes over the text before suggesting rhetorically: 'If anyone wants to leave, over there is the door.' I marched straight out. For months afterwards, the supervisor continued calling to confirm 'The job is still open.' To me it was well and truly closed.

Calling friends and family would have offended the few principles I had left. Unemployed or not – and I was, for six months afterwards – friends and family were too precious to be exploited for financial gain. I am proud of what I did. But the conclusions I drew were way off beam. My conclusions were that:

- Taking advantage of contacts was immoral.
- Using your network for commercial purposes was inappropriate.
- The right thing to do was start from scratch and prosper through the sweat of your brow.

BUT – that is *not* the way to get lucky. **Luck is a function of opportunity** and needs to be given every chance to appear. Contacts are one of the great ways of doing so. Up to a point, the insurance company was right. Anyone who is in business – or is thinking of starting a business, or is self-employed, or simply wishes to generate a bit of extra income – should start by digging out their address book.

This would be a good time to revisit the list of goals in your notebook. Which of them could use a helping hand from Dame Fortune? Then, start from A in your list of names and addresses and don't stop until Z. Pick out anyone who might have the faintest interest in what you are doing in the area of your life you wish to enhance. It doesn't matter how long it's been since you last spoke to them or whether you think they might want to hear from you. Relax, you do not have to ring them all at once. I advise clients to organise their lists in order of probable warmth of welcome and call two people per week.

This exercise is about leverage. Everyone on your list has an address book of their own. Even the smallest networks consist of roughly twenty-five people. Many run into three figures. Your new venture might hold no interest to the person on the other end of the line but could be just the ticket for someone they know. This is how businesses grow. A tells B who tells C. I know of one corporate coach who has a clause in his contracts stating that clients **must write letters of commendation** if they are happy with the work that he does.

How many people do you think might be on your list – twenty, forty, sixty? The last time I did this exercise was just before the start of *The Challenge*. I was astounded to come up with 122 names.

One key point to remember about making your own luck is *you've got to persist*. I had intended to bask in the glory of my TV debut by taking the day off. Instead, sensing an opportunity that was too good to miss, I chained myself to the desk and rang round all 122 names on my list.

The first 96 were a dead end. Although many were pleased to hear my voice, these former acquaintances led me nowhere I wasn't already heading. By this stage, I was down to the long shots. It was four years since I'd last spoken to number 97 who was running a corporate-events company at the time. Not any more. She was now the PA to one of the UK's top sportsmen who had been thinking about finding a sports psychologist.

The sense of serendipity was overwhelming. Although it took several months for her people to talk to my people (i.e. put a date in our diaries), the sportsman and I finally got together and are currently exploring all manner of ways of working together.

This is not just about business. Building a network is one of the most effective ways of finding a partner. Everyone knows at least one couple who met through mutual acquaintances. You might not fancy X or Y, but they will have friends who just could be 'interesting'.

Set yourself up for luck – every day of your life

We've already covered what you should do before your head hits the pillow at night but it's the other end of the day that sets the tone.

At some point, we've all done it. The alarm goes off, one eye opens halfway and a groan escapes from your lips: 'Oh God, here we go again.' You might as well pull the covers over your head and go back to slumberland.

I am certainly not advocating that you leap out of bed, rip back the curtains and dance round the room (though my friend Pete Cohen recommends doing exactly that). However, starting each day with a serious case of 'The Grumps' does not sit well with your life coach (i.e. me). And lucky people emphatically don't do it.

A few months ago, I was invited to work with a new client in the Executive Recruitment industry. On arrival, I was surprised to learn that my 'client' was not one of the long list of candidates on their books but the boss of the agency itself. Lesley's issue turned out to be a hatred of mornings. She absolutely detested the start of the day – in her case at 5 a.m. – and this early-morning malaise was having a detrimental impact on her whole a.m. performance.

The feelings of dread kicked in before Lesley even went to bed the previous night (another form of this is what I call 'Sunday night-itis' – the sinking-stomach feeling that many people experience at the prospect of another week's work. If you suffer from that, the upcoming exercise is also for you).

I asked Lesley to get as clear as possible on what it was she hated about mornings. 'It's so dark in winter,' she sighed, 'I hardly seem to see daylight at all. Even in summer, I still expect to wake up and find it's pitch black outside. I get a knot in my tummy just thinking about it.'

That unpleasant feeling gave us a head start. I asked Lesley to close her eyes and imagine, as she'd described, waking up on a cold winter's morning. Once Lesley was completely associated (e.g. watching the action from *inside* her body), I suggested that she open the shutters and 'discover' a blazing sun overhead in the sky. Hot rays of sunshine were flooding through the bedroom and Lesley could hear the sound of birds chirping overhead. An ear-to-ear grin appeared on her face.

We then turned to the 'knot' inside Lesley's stomach. I wanted Lesley to picture the knot clearly in her mind and stretch it out as far as she could. Lesley's imagination did the rest. She converted the knot into a piece of elastic, turned that into a wafer-thin credit card and the card into a floppy piece of string. When she opened her eyes, all the discomfort had gone. For a short while, I asked Lesley to incorporate this exercise into her pre-bed routine especially if she felt the slightest tinge of 'morning sickness'.

Now that she had started to view mornings in a new light, I asked Lesley what she liked about that time of day. Once we'd got over the 'Nothing much comes to mind' phase, Lesley rattled off a list that was longer than she could ever have expected.

1. 'My husband – He makes a great cup of coffee.'
2. 'A big kiss from my son.'
3. The drive to work – 'There's almost no one on the road that early.'
4. Power shower – 'It really wakes me up.'
5. 'My dog running round the garden.'
6. 'Quiet quality to that time of day.'
7. First in the office – 'I get such a lot done.'
8. Suits – 'I do love a smart uniform!'

I showed Lesley her list. 'That's amazing,' she exclaimed. 'All of those are really important to me and they *only happen first thing*.' In NLP terms, this is called 'reframing'. Reframing changes the meaning of an experience and allows the subject to think about it differently. 'I think I'm starting to like mornings after all,' Lesley laughed. She was halfway there.

I wanted Lesley to take her reframing to a higher level. I challenged her to come up with three additional ways to make mornings better still. 'I love it when you stay in a hotel and they add berries to your cereal,' she nodded. 'I'll start doing that from tomorrow and maybe go for a walk before I get in the car. Also, I'll use the car phone to call a different friend each day on the way to work. I'm too tired to catch up at night and it will make the journey go even quicker.'

I met Lesley again two weeks later. She had clearly moved on (I arranged the session for 8 a.m. and she was bright as a button) but the Ghosts of Mornings Past still lingered. 'It's really odd,' she frowned. 'Mornings are now fun but I still can't bring myself to actually *like* them.' We were now in the arena of beliefs. From the information she gave me, it was clear that Lesley retained some strong views about mornings. 'I think of myself as more of a night person,' was one remark. 'Mornings are always an effort,' was another.

I took Lesley through the Changing Your Beliefs exercise from Session 4. We replaced her limiting beliefs with empowering substitutes (e.g. 'I'm at my best in the morning') and discovered the historical source of her 'morning sickness' (she hated school).

Lesley now gets up at 4.45 a.m. The colleagues who brought me in to work with their boss told me she's a bundle of energy from first thing to last. They are not entirely sure this is a 'good thing'.

Say 'Yes' to the Universe

The most powerful word in the English language is 'no'. Nothing drains energy, hope or ambition with the same complete finality of a 'no'.

'No' is so final. 'No' is like the blade of a guillotine: sharp, cold and clinical. 'No' ends a discussion before it's begun. 'No' closes a door that 'maybe' leaves open.

I look back with enormous regret at some of the times I've used the word 'no': at the fun I missed, the work I could have done, the friends I might have met. 'No' is just too easy to say. I wish the word was longer so it gave people time to pause.

I am not a big enthusiast of coaching tapes. I am always losing the damn things down the side of the car seat and the vast majority of them recycle material you've already heard somewhere else. And I hate the part when the speaker says, 'Do not do this next exercise while in charge of a vehicle,' although they know full well 99% of tapes are being listened to in a car.

One I did like is by Susan Jeffers, author of *Feel the Fear and Do It Anyway*. (I know this is heresy, and the book is marvellous and she's sold 50 gadzillion copies, but, I'm sorry – that title is just so-o-o-o-o-o cheesy.) Back to the tape. One of the best parts features Susan recalling the period of her life when she was diagnosed with cancer. Faced with such a life-threatening situation, Susan consoled herself that at least she would receive the unconditional support of her long-time partner – who chose that very moment to announce he was leaving.

Even the great Susan Jeffers almost gave up. As she lay in her hospital bed, the overwhelming temptation was to slip quietly away. Then came the moment that changed her life. Susan Jeffers did not simply stop feeling sorry for herself – she made a conscious *decision*. Susan said 'Yes' to the universe, 'Yes' to the disease, 'Yes' to the treatment and 'Yes' to her future, *whatever it held*.

Susan Jeffers stopped resisting, resenting and blocking. She vowed to stop living in fear and play the hand she was dealt. Within a few weeks, her illness went in to remission. A few weeks after that, a new partner appeared whom she would ultimately marry. Susan Jeffers had replaced a 'No' with a 'Yes'.

Of course, not all such stories have happy endings.

Dreadful things happen, they really do. Not everyone recovers from cancer. People suffer grievous reversals of emotional, familial or financial fortune. It is part of my job to counsel clients going through such traumas. And what I urge them to do, as gently as I am able, is *mourn*.

One of the cruellest aspects of modern society is our attitude towards grief. Grief, to insensitive minds, is viewed as a weakness that must be overcome. As a piece of useless advice, 'Pull yourself together' takes quite some beating. It is the very last thing I want my clients to do. Mourning is natural, mourning is essential, **mourning is the start of the process of healing.** It cannot be rushed. It most certainly cannot be missed out altogether.

Susan Jeffers mourned the onset of illness and the loss of her relationship. Both were, by any standard, devastating blows. Susan gave herself permission to mourn, space to come to terms with her grief and room for fresh perspective to enter. With perspective came wisdom. Susan Jeffers said 'Yes' to the Universe. It would be a turning point in her life.

Lucky people understand how to roll with the punches without going down for the count. When life takes them to places they would rather not go, they get curious instead of livid. They discover that the diversion was – by a strange 'coincidence' – exactly where they needed to go but would never have chosen if they'd been at the wheel.

Say 'Yes' to the Universe! This is such a powerful thought. It's one I drill and drill and drill again into all my coaching clients – especially sportsmen. The two greatest English sporting triumphs of the last fifty years have one thing in common – the opposition equalised in the very last minute.

If West Germany had not scored with 30 seconds remaining in the 1966 World Cup, England centre-forward Geoff Hurst would not have (through his equalising goal) notched up his famous hat trick. Hurst will always be grateful they did. Manager Alf Ramsey simply told his players they would win all over again. They said 'Yes' to the Universe.

The same was true of England's rugby heroes when Australia drew level in the closing moments of the 2003 World Cup final. Coach Clive Woodward's strategy reflected the same approach.

Contrast both reactions with soccer's Euro 2000 final in which France drew level against Italy with virtually the last kick of the game. Several of the Italian team later conceded that this was the moment they knew they would lose. They said 'No' to the Universe.

Lucky people are, above all, resilient. I do not mean those who enjoy spasmodic moments of good fortune but those who soar from one triumph to the next. They are not waylaid by obstacles, rebuffs or disappointments. They accept that success brings with it reversals of fortune and *actively welcome the challenge*. 'Business,' one such told me, 'wouldn't be business without problems.'

People who know that I work with high achievers, and want to become part of their world, grill me for hours on what they need to do and become. I tell them to say 'Yes' to the Universe. I tell them to learn the skills of resilience. **Finally, I tell them to switch on their antennae.**

There are no coincidences. When one enters your life,

pay attention. When a friend or a book or a movie you'd been thinking about just the other day just 'happens' to appear, do not walk away. In there, somewhere, is an opportunity or a message. The Universe will help you get where you're going if you just stop being such a know-all. I'll prove it. How did you meet your partner? How close did you come to never meeting him or her? Was it a party you almost didn't go to, a bar you happened to wander into or a chance encounter in a place where you wouldn't normally have been? *Almost everyone meets in this fashion.*

I 'met' my future wife as I was leaving a barbecue – literally walking out of the door on my way home. As I was in a hurry (I was going to watch athletics!), I didn't stay to chat but asked a friend to get her number. She 'just happened' to be the sort of person who was intrigued by someone with that kind of nerve. Mind you, she's given me a hard time about it ever since. Fifteen seconds later and I'd have missed her – and I could so easily have left thirty seconds earlier or been looking the other way. But I wasn't. Because there are no coincidences. And taking advantage of coincidence is saying 'Yes' to the Universe.

Saying 'Yes' to the Universe puts you where you need to be. Saying 'No' to the Universe makes you a victim. The music that victims hear in their head is a tune with a thousand variations on the theme of 'Poor Me'.

You are not that. You are better than that. You are more than that. You are lucky.

Session Summary

1. What you are is what you get. Conduct a seven-day experiment during which you give away what you want.
2. Calculate your Luck Baseline. What does it tell you?
3. Go over the events of each day before heading for bed. Replay your five highlights.
4. Take responsibility for the successes you are seeking to create. Contact two old friends or business associates each week and see what opportunities arise.
5. Say 'Yes' to the Universe.

SESSION 8
Decisions Made Easy

Decisions can be scary. Decisions are scary because you might get them wrong. And if you get them wrong, all sorts of consequences might ensue, consequences that are simply too awful to contemplate. So, you don't take decisions.

If you don't take decisions, you stay where you are. You don't *like* where you are, you want to be somewhere else but you can't get somewhere else without taking a decision. But decisions are scary because you might be wrong. So you stay where you are. Your indecision is final. Both ways you lose.

Catastrophic Fantasies are part of the equation. Faced with a decision, the consequences of getting it wrong snowball through the mind. Horrendous scenarios play out in Technicolor detail. People see, hear and feel (especially *feel*) all the ghastly repercussions until doing nothing becomes the safer option.

Remember *The Challenge*? What worked was having answers to the question 'What Will I Gain If I Succeed?' Taking decisions demands the same mindset – 'What Will I Gain If This Decision Is Right?' What I will have, what I will do, what I will *be* if I take my courage in both hands. Sadly, the only reason that many people take decisions **at all** is when the pain of staying where they are becomes so unbearable that 'anything is better than this'.

Once again, the price you pay is ghastly. The pattern is set for all meaningful decisions. Years go by in which you complain of staying stuck (through no fault of your own, of course) but feel powerless to do anything about it. One of the many remarkable aspects of the human character is our seemingly *infinite capacity to tolerate the intolerable* which we do until breaking point is finally reached. At this point, we tell ourselves, once again, that 'Anything is better than this' and finally move on.

A lot of people will be squirming in their seats after reading that – for them – hugely uncomfortable last paragraph. My question is this. Have you suffered enough yet? Are you ready to do something about it? Here comes that mantra – *confidence is a relationship of trust between 'you' and 'you'*. Refusing to act is for cowards. If you can't even trust yourself to take a decision, how can you grow?

No one is immune from difficulties with decisions

One of my clients is a champion boxer. Rippling with muscle from head to toe, this warrior has no problem walking into the ring in front of 30,000 hostile spectators. But reluctance to take a decision almost cost him his career.

I was called in to work with the Champ before a big fight. The brief was vague (it almost always is) and

I assumed we'd be talking about such matters as breathing techniques, focus under pressure or powers of mental recovery. Far from it. This legend of the ring could not decide whether or not to break up with his girlfriend. They'd been together for six years. The passion had gone and so had the sex, companionship and respect – or so he told me.

I got the distinct impression that his seconds couldn't have cared less. What they did care about was the Champ's half-hearted preparation for the upcoming fight and the big pay days they were in danger of losing.

The boxer was actually a big softie. All his ferocity and aggression were reserved for the ring. When he left the arena, the Champ did what he was told – especially at home. I got the feeling he liked it. This syndrome is amazingly common. Giants of industry, entertainment and sport spend all day barking instructions at minions; they then go home at night, walk through the door and are told what to do. Letting someone else take charge for a change is a relief – until it no longer is.

Postponing decisions is never the answer

We all know divorce is rife. I've seen dozens of different reasons cited for the collapse of the hallowed institution formerly known as marriage and none convinces me at all. Sometimes, I grant you, it comes down to money. And, yes, sometimes he really is having an affair with 'her three doors down'. But, most of the time, his family, her family, pressures of work, his snoring, her nagging – all of these are little more than red herrings.

By far – *by far* – the biggest reason most people get divorced, or split up, or pack their bags and go home to Mum is because one partner or the other goes through a process of *change*. That oft-voiced cry, 'You are not the man I married,' is actually spot on. The mistake that partners so often make, with the inevitable death of their relationship, is resisting that change. Couples who stay together do so by adapting to, or tolerating, or (for those who hit pay dirt in the shape of their soul mate) *encouraging* change in each other.

Here's the critical shift in thinking that helps keep couples together. Change is natural; standing still is unnatural. Change keeps a relationship breathing; stagnation cuts off the air supply. One is moving forward while the other is stuck.

Relationship therapy is about understanding change and exploring how each partner can be encouraged or supported in their own efforts to evolve. It is the attempt to preserve 'what we once had' in aspic that leads inexorably to disaster.

That was what had happened to the boxer. He and his girlfriend had been together since his early years as a pro. While he concentrated on separating opponents from their limbs, she maintained a stable home base. When he walked through the door after a hard day's training, she wore the trousers.

The Champ was no longer a novice. He had gained confidence, status and self-respect. He did not appreciate being told what to do in his own home. By contrast, his partner appeared to have ignored, or was simply unaware of, her own need for development. She had stagnated. Stagnation is boring and he wanted out. My client complained that he felt suffocated: his girlfriend was moody, clingy and resentful of his success. I suggested that pictures of her boyfriend on the town with lap dancers gave her sound cause for irritation. My observation was not well received.

The Champ was convinced he was ready to move on. But, for whatever reason, the decision to split was proving beyond him. I wondered what was holding him back. He told me he'd come from a broken home and love in childhood was strictly rationed. His parents had operated on the reward-and-punishment principle, withholding affection from unruly, disruptive or disobedient children (i.e. he and his siblings most of the time). Whatever her faults, his girlfriend's love was unconditional. My client was concerned that he might never find such devotion again.

In a way, he was right. Relationships don't come with guarantees; you can't take them back if they break. One of the main causes of commitment phobia among men (why do I feel female readers paying particular attention to this sentence?) is the lack of any such guarantee. Men need certainty. If your chap keeps pulling back from the brink of commitment, I suggest you explain that no one ever did know (not even Nan and Gramps who've been together since World War I) that their relationship was certain to endure. The male of the species is loath to risk failure even when the odds may actually be in favour of success.

Our session was coming to an end and I'd barely begun. I explained that we'd need to go through a decision-making process that would deliver a conclusion one way or the other. In addition, I would want to clear up the detritus of childhood in order to allow the client to distinguish love from need.

A follow-up session was arranged for a few days before the big bout. I was concerned that this would be too late to allow the Champ sufficient time to enter the ring with a clear head, but was told training schedules had to take precedence. In the event, that second session was cancelled. The promoter demanded the boxer's presence at a press conference in a last-minute attempt to put more bums on seats. The Champ lost the fight.

In an ill-advised effort to take matters into his own hands (on the advice of his manager!), the boxer had sat his girlfriend down and suggested they split. She burst into tears, he gave her a hug, all resolve promptly disappeared and they thrashed the issue back and forth all night. He went training next morning on virtually no sleep. His performance in the gym disintegrated. Instead of putting all his attention where it needed to go – into the fight – he allowed doubts about the relationship to churn round his mind.

At the summit of world sport, the difference between winning and losing is minuscule. Only those at their peak of physical and psychological fitness can hope to prevail. The boxer was beaten before he'd even weighed in. Defeat only made matters worse. Recriminations raged between promoter and manager, manager and boxer, and boxer and partner. He blamed her for not letting him go; she blamed him for leading her up the garden path.

As far as I know, the couple are still together. He calls me now and again, complains about the relationship and goes home to the partner he'd rather not be with. Meanwhile, he's waiting for a rematch that may never come and she's waiting for wedding bells she'll almost certainly never hear.

Postponing decisions is undeniably tempting. With any luck, fate will intervene and save you the trouble (for instance, by taking the decision out of your hands). The funny thing is that fate usually *does* intervene – but almost never in the way that you'd hoped.

Build your mind muscle

> 'The more we live by our intellect, the less we understand the meaning of life.'
>
> LEO TOLSTOY

The ability to take decisions is a muscle. And like all muscles, it requires regular exercise or withers away from disuse. I see plenty of puny decision-making muscles. Their owners seem to forget they have them at all. 'I can't make a decision to save my life,' they laugh, as if there's nothing they can do about it and, what the hell, they'll live with it anyway. My glare usually wipes the smile from their face.

Everyone is capable of taking decisions – big ones, small ones and those of indeterminate width. For once, size actually doesn't matter. Taking decisions is a habit. Big decisions are easier to make if you get into the habit of taking small ones. The key is to *begin*. And the way to begin is to become aware of the decisions you are already making every day of your life. For instance:

Corn Flakes or Rice Krispies?
Tesco's or Sainsbury's?
BBC or ITV?
Bath or shower?
Chocolate or fruit?
Go to work or take the day off?

Everyone takes decisions all the time, they just aren't aware that they do so. Even the smallest decision is still a decision, and these choices prove that the mindset needed is still in there somewhere. Clients are rarely convinced by this argument. 'But these are "no brainers",' they protest. 'I don't think, I just do them.' My point precisely.

Decisions divide into two categories: logical and instinctive. Logical decisions are those you take after hours of contemplative thought. These are the ones that go round and round and drive you crazy and make you wander about the house at four in the morning. This is not a helpful process. Instinctive decisions are the ones you take because they just 'feel' right; you somehow seem to *know* what to do. We will talk about those in a moment. Logical and instinctive decisions are fundamentally different mental processes that should be used at different times. Getting them confused is a prime cause of decision-making gridlock.

The rest of this chapter examines these two different forms of taking decisions. But, in the meantime . . .

Make as many decisions as you can.

You heard me. Go out of your way to exercise your decision-making muscle. Put it in a singlet and get it on the treadmill. Take decisions wherever you go – *decide* what to wear, *decide* what to do, *decide* what to eat, *decide* who to see – *and stick to them*! Do not change your mind. Take a decision, whatever it is, and hold with it.

How many decisions can you take in the next hour, the next minute, *right now*? Don't give too much thought to whether these decisions are 'right' or 'wrong'; at this stage, that isn't the point. I guarantee you will feel stronger, more confident, more *alive* purely for getting in the habit of deciding. As I said at the start of this session, it is fear of consequences that prevents decisions being taken in the first place . . . which stops you taking them when you really need to . . . which inhibits your self-esteem and makes it even harder to take them. So, we'll start with the easy stuff (e.g. what to eat) and work our way up as confidence builds.

Now *fast-forward to this evening*. How many decisions did you take? Don't guess, make a list – five, ten, twenty? Actually, the number isn't that important – as long as it's greater than nought.

I want you to take *more* decisions tomorrow. One

Decisions Made Easy

more is fine, two is better, ten is outstanding. Please gain an increasing awareness of your ability to take decisions. You can do it, you really can do it – *you are doing it*!

You are not weak and you never were; just out of practice. The difference is crucial. The difference is *everything*. Your decision-making muscles are no longer flatlining. Signs of life are apparent but more power is needed. Let's turn up the voltage.

Learn to use your sixth sense

'The intuitive mind is a sacred gift and the rational mind is a faithful servant. We have created a society that honours the servant and has forgotten the gift.'
ALBERT EINSTEIN

In May 2005, a university student from Whitley Bay in Northumberland sauntered into the centre of town. Sarah Cockings (21) liked to play the lottery at her local post office because sister Alex manned the terminal. Unlike so many punters, who use the dates of their birthdays or the ages of their kids, Sarah had always opted to play Lucky Dip. This time she didn't. Walking up to the counter, Sarah had what she would later describe as a 'funny feeling'. For the first time since she had started playing the lottery four years earlier, Sarah used her instinct and selected the numbers herself.

She won £1 million. 'Normally I just go up to the Lotto terminal that Alex runs,' Sarah recalled, 'and ask her for three Lucky Dips. For some strange reason I had a feeling that I should choose my numbers this week for the first time.' Trusting her instincts paid handsome dividends. Pocketing her seven-figure sum, Sarah went back to university to finish her degree in social work, though not before splashing out on a car.

We have six senses not five. Five we use and one is ignored – which is a pity as it might be the best of them all. It wasn't always like this. Back in the days of dinosaurs, loincloths and men who said 'ug', the human race lived on its instincts. Men and women ate when they were hungry, had sex when they were horny and reacted without analysing every small issue to death.

Then thought set in. Thought became the predominant driver for human activity. Before any action could be taken, it had to be redirected via the brain for official sanctioning. While thought became a power-mad bureaucrat, instinct fell out of favour. What had once come naturally was displaced by cogitation. The baton had been passed from 'I am' to 'I think therefore I am (but let me think about it)'.

Control became paramount. Only the checks and balances of thought could ensure that each decision was debated with all due process. The age of the Control Freak had dawned.

In the twenty-first century, we live under a totalitarian regime. Thought is a tyrant that will stomach no rivals. George Orwell – creator of 'Big Brother is watching you' in his book *1984* – almost had it right, except that 'Big Brother' is inside us, not out. We have become brains on legs. The mind barks out a series of instructions that must be obeyed at all times. Instinct is dismissed as risky, fanciful or just plain *imaginary*.

I am not advocating a return to the Jurassic age (though a Theme Park might be fun). No one would dispute that the massive advances in science, medicine and technology were principally generated by brainpower. But thought is not the best tool for every job. Always taking thought as your starting point, no matter what, will not work because that is not what it was constructed to do.

In Session 1, I explained how to reconnect with your animal. Whichever creature you are doesn't furrow its brow before deciding whether to eat or sleep or sunbathe. It doesn't gather in a huddle with other members of the species and deliberate on when to head south for winter. It just *knows*.

You know more than you know. You have just forgotten you know it. Because you've forgotten, you have also become disconnected from the mechanism that drives your sixth sense. In order to improve the quality of our decisions – to take them faster, better and with greater certainty – we need to reawaken our instincts.

You can do this. You have done – on many occasions.

HEART OR HEAD?

- Grab a piece of paper and two coloured pens (different colours!).
- Write a list in your notebook of all the decisions you've ever made. Go back as far as you like,

make the list as long as you can. Don't sweat it –
*you don't have to decide which ones to include or
leave out!*

- Just get them all down – those that mattered, those
  that didn't and those that fall somewhere between.
  It might be deciding to:
    - learn Spanish
    - convert to Buddhism
    - play the guitar
    - eat guacamole
    - go to Paraguay
    - have your ears pierced
    - go out with Desmond
    - buy this mobile not that one
- Take at least 5 minutes.
- If your list comprises fewer than 50 items, you are
  clearly not trying and we may have to consider
  detention.

★

★

★

★

★

★

★

★

Well done.

- Now, go through the list one decision at a time.
- Please take the first coloured pen and place a tick beside all the decisions you took on the basis of *thought*: those you ruminated over at length before reaching a conclusion. *It doesn't matter whether those decisions turned out to be right or wrong.*
- Now pick up the second pen, go back through the list and place a tick beside those decisions you took on *instinct*. You just knew what to do and you did it. Once again, it doesn't matter if those decisions turned out to be right or wrong. Yes, there will be grey areas. It may be that you had an instinctive reaction, reverted to thought, then took a decision. As long as thinking did not change your mind, that one counts as instinctive.
- Count up the ticks and keep a note of the totals.

Here's where it gets interesting (what do you mean it wasn't already?). I know I said it doesn't matter if the decisions you took were right or wrong. Now, it does.

- Go back through your 'Thinking' list and count the number of decisions that turned out to be correct.
- Once you have a figure, convert that into a percentage (e.g. 7 out of 20 = 35%).
- Repeat the process for instinct.
- Count the correct decisions and do the percentage calculation.

If the outcome is the same as most of my clients, you'll assume you've done it wrong. You'll huff and puff, go through it again and reach the same result. You'll scratch your head and give me a look of 'How can that be?'

Instinctive decisions – those that are taken in the bat of an eye – always come out on top. In fact, they win by a mile. Instinct works. Our instincts are fabulous. More often than not, they know exactly what to do. We've trained ourselves not to listen. We prefer to obey the 'voice of reason'. As reason 'sounds' so reasonable, our instincts are overridden.

But intuition is a persistent so and so. No matter how little attention you give it, the whisper of instinct never completely goes silent. It is always there, providing you with a gentle tap on the shoulder, a helpful nudge in just the direction you really know, deep down, you ought to be going.

MAKE THE MOST OF YOUR INNER WHISPER

Our sixth sense is every bit as powerful, every bit as real as the other five. The fact that we cannot see it or hear it, smell or touch or taste it makes it no less part of what we are.

I teach my clients to use their intuition actively. Once they have completed the above exercise, little further persuasion is needed. They have had enough of all that contemplation, all that deliberation, all that *angst*. It wouldn't be so bad if it actually worked.

Nothing should be easier than instinctive behaviour. After all, it's what we're born to do. Unfortunately, someone has interfered with our software and a new program is needed. Rebooting your instincts demands putting heart before head. In this clash of the titans, the heart has been overpowered. Even in the one sphere where the heart has traditionally held sway – romance – decisions about who to have or to hold have been left to our pragmatic heads.

It is time to reopen your heart. When faced with a choice, ask yourself: 'How will I *feel* if I do this?' or 'Will it make me happy (or not)?'

A reminder. This is not namby-pamby, touchy-feely, happy-clappy, wishy-washy, off-with-the-fairies behaviour. You are not doing this out of some misguided sense of internal political correctness. You have instincts for a reason. As you have already established, they are hugely effective at what they do. They just don't get the chance to do it very often. This puts that right.

You won't have to wait long to try it out. Next time you go shopping, dozens of opportunities will arise. Should I buy this red or white wine? Should I buy wine at all? It's a bit of an indulgence and I promised to cut down and . . .

Stop! This chatter is your head not your heart. You have fallen back into old habits by allowing thought to take charge. Deep breath, start again!

As I pointed out during our last session, thinking is the least effective method of obtaining your heart's desire. Unleash your potential by unlocking your instincts.

Knowledge + Instinct = Success

Dr Roger Wolman has known me since the age of 13. We shared a room together for two years at boarding school. Shortly after I'd started appearing as a radio pundit, Roger made an interesting observation. 'Never mind talking about sports psychology,' he declared; 'I don't know anyone whose predictions about sporting events are as accurate as yours. It's just something you've always been able to do.'

Roger had been round to watch a football match with me – a semifinal of the Carling Cup between Liverpool (his team) and Crystal Palace. The South London side were leading 1–0 from the first leg. 'Don't worry, Rodge,' I heard myself saying after barely five minutes. 'Liverpool will win 5–0.' And they did. Exactly 5–0.

Once the final whistle had blown, Roger asked if I had any other predictions. Actually I did. That weekend was the fourth round of the FA Cup and I harboured a sneaking suspicion that outsiders West Ham would beat red-hot favourites Manchester United. Roger guffawed. 'No way,' he said, 'that's ridiculous.'

'I also fancy Arsenal to beat Queen's Park Rangers by six goals at least,' I added. Realising he was clearly in the presence of an idiot, Roger left.

Arsenal played QPR on Saturday afternoon. I went for a nap before the game started and was woken up by my wife around five. 'Any shocks in the Cup?' I asked. 'No,' she replied. 'Though Arsenal did beat poor QPR six-nil.' My blood ran cold. Even I was shocked to get that one bang on.

Roger rang me that night. 'Well done,' he conceded,

'but you must admit West Ham have absolutely no chance against Man United.' Logic told me Roger was right. By the time we'd discussed the relative strengths of the teams – the fact that United were top of the Premiership while West Ham had not won away all season – I was forced to concede this time I'd got it wrong.

But I hadn't. West Ham won at Old Trafford 1–0, pulling off the biggest Cup shock in years. On reflection, I realised that Roger had a point. A disproportionate number of my predictions did seem to come true. I could do it in golf too. My tips for tournaments invariably finished in the top five (not bad in a field of 150) and often took home the trophy at the end of four rounds. This was more intriguing than I'd realised; but, before jacking in my career to take up residence in a bookies, I needed to know more.

I was also better at some sports than others. I'd been to the Royal Ascot racecourse five times and lost money on four. My trips to the greyhounds were also a fiasco. My instincts were effective in some areas but seriously fallible in others. What was going on?

I eventually stumbled across a book by the American writer, Malcolm Gladwell. *Blink* begins with the jaw-dropping story of how the Getty Museum in California paid $10 million for a Greek statue dating from the sixth century BC.

Before agreeing to purchase the statue, a geologist spent two days examining the artefact with a high-resolution stereomicroscope. Core samples were subsequently subjected to inspection by electron microscopes, electron microphobes (I've no idea what they are, either), X-ray diffraction and mass spectrometry. Analysis concluded that the statue was genuine. Delighted to have captured such a rare artefact, the Getty Museum handed over the funds and the statue went on public display in the autumn of 1986. Art critics published glowing reviews and visitors queued around the block to view the piece.

Evelyn Harrison was a world expert on Greek sculpture. She took one look at the statue and 'just knew' it was fake. Georgios Donatas agreed. Head of the Archaeological Society of Athens, Donatas exclaimed, 'Anyone who has ever seen a sculpture coming out of the ground could tell that thing had never been in the ground.'

They were right. Further investigation began to raise doubts about the provenance of documents authenticating the statue. It turned out to have been made in a forger's workshop just a few years earlier.

Elsewhere in the book, Gladwell cites many other occasions when instincts prove to be highly misleading. The conclusion he reaches is that instinct can only be relied upon if it is supported by expertise and experience.

The reason my soccer and golf predictions tend to pan out is because I work in those sports. I know how footballers and golf pros think under pressure and this adds weight to my instincts. This is also why I will always lose money on dogs, horses and the Eurovision Song Contest. Bookmakers depend on your guesswork for profits. In order to redress the odds in your favour, expertise is essential which you generally won't have.

Instinct may be marginally preferable to knowledge

on its own, but I strongly advise caution. As soon as instinct is coloured by need (e.g. I must win to pay the rent/clothe my kids), the mixture becomes tainted. True instinct has no compulsion or price.

When thought is needed – how to make decisions that stick

Of course, instinct is not the only way of taking decisions. Despite the emphasis of this session thus far, reasoned argument remains the foundation of meaningful choice. However, most internal arguments are anything but reasonable. The two sides of an argument bounce backwards and forwards across the skull like a game of Ping-Pong until one side hits a winner – or the other gives in because they simply can't stand the noise.

I want to show you a process that is far more effective. Over the years, I have developed a step-by-step method of taking decisions that not only cuts out the din but delivers a solid conclusion. It seems to work for all kinds of decisions – large or small – and is easy to remember and do on your own. This one falls into the 'that makes sense so I'll probably do it' category.

A dilemma that comes up time and again in my clients' lives is whether to move on. The merry-go-round of football's transfer market brings a flood of mercenaries . . . er, clients . . . to my door, uncertain whether to accept an offer (that hasn't yet officially been made, and I mustn't tell anyone about it – especially the manager, but their agent has been approached by someone from another club and they don't know what to do) and could I help?

The corporate world isn't much different. Even long-standing members of staff find their loyalties stretched beyond breaking point by the offer of a king's ransom from a competitor. In both cases, much the same issues arise – relocation vs salary, new challenge vs 'I quite like what I do now'.

THE ULTIMATE DECISION-MAKING TOOL

This exercise usually takes around 45 minutes and includes a couple of loo/snack/fag breaks. It works equally well for decisions about relationships or new cars or holidays or jobs. To illustrate each stage, I will use the example of a client who was a Deputy Manager from the nightclub industry whom I worked with when he was offered the chance to run his own club. For you to really grasp how it can work for you, you should apply it to a situation in your life that requires a decision. Of course, situations will sometimes arise that present a variety of options or outcomes to choose from. However, for the purpose of this exercise, pick one that (at least) seems to need a simple 'Shall I or shan't I?' or 'Shall I do A or B?' decision.

Step 1. What do I know? The main reason that decisions are so hard to take (doh!) is because you don't know what to do. And part of what stops you knowing what to do is the knowledge that you don't have. Fine. What DO you know about the situation, though? Come on, it's plenty. Make a list.

I asked the nightclub manager what he could tell me about his new employers, new place of work, colleagues, customers, hours, terms and conditions etc. By the time we'd finished, it filled several pages.

If we were talking about whether or not to get married (yes, the big one), I'd be asking you to list what you know (that is 'know' not 'presume') about the person you are planning to spend the rest of your life with. What are his or her interests, foibles, strengths, weaknesses, good points, bad points, history, background? What do you love about him or her and what drives you nuts?

Do not draw any conclusions at this stage (though you will be tempted)! Stick to the facts and keep emotion at arm's length. It is almost certainly emotion that has got you into this fix of indecision so let's not open the door any wider.

All we are attempting to do, at this stage, is tease out preliminary information, much of which will be reused and all of which will be supplemented as we go on.

So there it is. Yes, I realise it doesn't make things all that much easier. Wild suggestion – stop being so impatient! On we go.

Step 2. *What do you stand for?* Which are the values that you hold dearest and describe you as a person? Would you put ambition above loyalty? Security before adventure? Freedom ahead of hard work?

There are no right or wrong answers. Knowing your values – what matters to you – provides a heightened degree of personal awareness. Awareness supplies the ammunition for purpose. Once you become aware of your purpose, you know what to do.

Take a look through the list of values below. It is long but not comprehensive; please feel free to add others that would provide a more fully rounded selection in your case. Once you have scanned through the list – carefully –

Select the 10 values that are most important to you:

Accomplishment	Diversity
Achievement	Education
Adventure	Efficiency
Beauty	Equality
Calm	Excellence
Challenge	Fairness
Change	Faith
Collaboration	Family
Commitment	Flair
Communication	Freedom
Community	Friendship
Competence	Fun
Competition	Generosity
Concern for others	Global view
Conservation	Goodness
Creativity	Gratitude
Decisiveness	Hard work
Determination	Harmony
Discipline	Honesty
Discovery	Honour

Innovation	Respect
Integrity	Responsibility
Justice	Results
Knowledge	Risk
Leadership	Security
Love	Selflessness
Loyalty	Self-reliance
Meaning	Service
Mobility	Sincerity
Money	Skill
Non-violence	Speed
Openness	Spirit
Patriotism	Stability
Peace	Status
Perfection	Strength
Persistence	Style
Personal growth	Teamwork
Pioneering spirit	Timeliness
Pleasing others	Tolerance
Pleasure	Tradition
Positive attitude	Tranquillity
Power	Trust
Privacy	Truth
Progress	Unity
Reliability	Variety
Resourcefulness	Wisdom

Do you have your ten? Good. Now I want you to reduce it to four. Yes, I know – 'it took me long enough to come down to ten and now you want me to reduce it to four. Next you'll be asking me to pick out just one!' No I won't. Four is fine. Choose the four values that sum up what is truly important to you.

This is your special values formula. Know it, feel it, take time to appreciate what you stand for. Whatever decision you reach must, *must*, **must** be in line with this list.

Step 3. *What are your alternatives?* It's time to start putting the decision-making process into practice. Refer back to your own situation, the dilemma you've picked from your own life. Write down Alternative A at the top of one sheet of paper and Alternative B at the top of another.

In the case of my nightclub manager, he had been offered a promotion from Deputy Head of the hippest venue in town to General Manager of a rival's (let's be generous) moth-eaten dive. After years of yearning to run his own club, this offer had come out of the blue.

Step 4. *Alternative A – advantages* Take the Alternative A sheet and list the advantages of making that choice in the *short* and *long* term. Don't rush. Allow any lingering fog to clear and advantages will soon start popping into your head. Crib the info you generated during Step 1 if you have to.

Again, try and stay neutral. Most people begin this exercise secretly expecting to choose one or other alternative. Avoid falling into that trap and you will find it far more rewarding.

Option A for the nightclub manager involved taking the new job. Short-term advantages included a healthy pay rise, a company car and a growing reputation as a 'face about town'. Long-term benefits included self-respect and the chance to manage more salubrious clubs.

Step 5. Alternative A – disadvantages Take Alternative A and list the disadvantages of that choice in the short and long term. Switch sides and play devil's advocate. What are the drawbacks of Option A? What will I have to do that I'd rather not, thank you very much all the same? Where will it take me that I may not want to be? Who will I have to work or live with that I'd rather avoid?

For my manager, the short-term disadvantages included having to move home and leaving the company of valued colleagues. Contemplating the longer-term downside produced a wholly unexpected revelation. My client realised he had never intended the nightclub industry to be more than a transient stop in his professional journey.

Step 6. Time out Have a break to clear your head. Long enough for a walk or cup of tea (mine is white with one sugar).

Step 7. Alternative B – advantages Move on to Alternative B and list the advantages of that choice in the short and long term. You know the ropes. Take a dispassionate view and write them all down. Don't cheat. Even if this choice appears less attractive at first, give it just as much time to reveal its hidden charms. Of course, if you're still struggling after ten minutes, that may be a clue.

Step 8. Alternative B – disadvantages List the disadvantages of alternative B in the short and long term. Alternative B for the nightclub manager was staying where he was. Short-term advantages included continuing to work in a town he knew well and not having to move (i.e. the flipside of Step 5). Long-term benefits included the possibility of inheriting the General Manager's job in due course and his existing employers subsidising an MBA (Master of Business Administration) course.

The short-term downside of staying put required little thought. It included damage to health (he'd been ill for months) and 'forcing myself to come into work every day'. The long-term disadvantages were worse: 'I'd lose all self-respect and have to finally face my lack of ambition.'

Step 9. Take a l-o-o-o-o-o-ng break Do not contemplate, think about or dwell upon your alternatives for at least two hours. If you can leave it longer, even overnight, so much the better. Have lunch, go for a stroll, take a bath, watch a movie – I really don't care.

And nor should you. The hard work is done. Rest easy in the knowledge that once we pick up the process, the decision will be a no-brainer. You may think you know what that decision will be. Maybe you do, maybe you don't. If you do, that's fine. If you don't, that's absolutely fine too. You soon will.

Step 10. Have you had a break? A proper break? You should return to the material in a completely neutral frame of mind. Putting distance – i.e. time – between yourself and the information allows you to look all the 'evidence' you've assembled through a fresh pair of eyes. Read all of your answers again. Recall your values before you start reading. Rediscover the advantages and disadvantages of each option in turn and allow any new ones to appear.

Step 11. Decision time The time for reflection is over. In the cold light of day, having weighed up all the evidence, which is the option you have decided to take? Which one feels right? It may not be the option you wanted to choose or expected to choose when we began this process. It may leave you with some explaining to do and uncomfortable conversations to endure but:

a) The decision is clearly in line with your values.
b) It feels like the right thing to do.
c) Deep down, your instincts agree.

Step 12. Double-checking Let's bolt the back door. In order to banish any lingering doubts, I'm going to guide you through a quick visualisation.

Close your eyes (after reading through this exercise, obviously). Imagine you are back in the cinema we left in Session 4. You remember the one – where you transformed limiting beliefs into empowering beliefs. Go there now. Pick a seat quickly as the feature is about to begin. It's called *What My Life Will Be Like In Six Months' Time Having Gone Through With This Decision*. Run the movie please, Mr Projectionist!

What do you see? How are things panning out? How is life different? How are you thinking, behaving and acting differently? Stop watching the screen for a few seconds. Are you enjoying the film? Do you feel good about what you're seeing? Are you pleased with the decision you've taken? If so, step into the action. Stay as long as you like and enjoy the life that awaits you. Come back to your seat when the scene has played out.

The next movie is almost ready. This one is called *What My Life Will Be Like In Twelve Months' Time Having Gone Through With This Decision*. Same deal. Don't second-guess what you're about to see, allow the scene to unfold in its own time. What will you be doing this time next year if you stick with the decision you've made? Where will you be? Who will you be with? What will you be experiencing, learning, enjoying, discovering? As before, step into the movie if you like.

The third film moves the timeline further forward still. This one is called called *What My Life Will Be Like In Two Years' Time Having Gone Through With This Decision*. You should see some really big changes now. The full benefits of the decision you've taken will be apparent including all those long-term advantages.

Our triple bill is complete. You've now seen how the decision will impact your life. Is this what you want? Does what you have just seen confirm the wisdom of your choice? You should have no doubts left at all.

Purely for the sake of completeness, I am going to give you the chance to watch another three movies. One, however, will almost certainly be enough.

The first of these films is called *What My Life Will Be Like In Six Months' Time If I Take The Alternative Option*. Assume you made the alternative choice. You read through the notes and this was the option you picked. It may not seem as exciting or liberating or powerful, but this was the decision you went for. Run the film. It's six months from now and this is the life your decision has produced. How do you feel about what you are watching? Better or worse than before? Does this movie fill you with hope or dread?

A second exercise is rarely needed. This first 18-rated preview is usually more than enough to underline the wisdom of your choice. We'll keep the 12- and 24-month versions in a locked vault where no one can see them. After all, they are a bit scary.

Session Summary

1. Build up your decision-making muscles. Get into the habit of taking as many decisions as you can as often as possible. Notice yourself becoming more decisive.

2. Trust your instincts. Use your hunches. Add the layers of knowledge that will make your instincts more effective.

3. Think about the values you picked out. Your values provide a profound indicator of what really matters to you. Use your values to guide decisions from now on.

4. Practise the decision-making strategy from this session. Once it is committed to memory, the whole process takes no more than 10–15 minutes. Make it work. Taking decisions you can trust provides a dramatic boost in levels of self-confidence.

The Mindset of Champions

He was born in the fishing city of Setubal in Portugal. He was not especially academic or gifted or athletic. But he was different. From a young age, he seemed to sense it. So did everyone around him. His father was the goalkeeper for Vittoria FC, the local football club. However, the son wasn't good enough make the footballing grade and enrolled on a Business Course. He lasted precisely one day. Undeterred by taking a wrong turn, he opted for a Physical Education qualification instead. Most afternoons, he took charge of Sebutal's Under-18 squad, training on a pitch with more weeds than grass.

The young man had a talent for languages and accepted a job as an interpreter with Sporting Lisbon FC. The club had recruited an English manager called Bobby Robson who spoke barely a word of Portuguese. Robson was impressed. The interpreter was loyal, ambitious and eager to learn. He also had a flair for tactics. When Robson left for Porto FC, he took his interpreter along and promoted him to Assistant Manager.

Porto won the Championship two years in a row and the pair were invited to take charge at Barcelona FC. Further success followed including two Spanish Cup triumphs and a UEFA Cup victory. Robson *returned to England to take the helm as manager of Newcastle United but, this time, decided against taking his assistant with him.*

The young man ploughed on. Within a year, he was recruited to manage Benefica FC, the undisputed giants of Portuguese soccer. Nine games into the job, he was fired. The opportunity of a lifetime had come and gone.

Still refusing to be blown off course, he joined an unheralded side called Uniao de Leiria and stunned Portuguese soccer by taking the minnows to third in the league. Benefica asked him to return but the young man declined. He joined Porto FC instead and announced, before the first game of the season had kicked off, that his side would win the league. They did. And the next season too. And the UEFA Cup. Then, the greatest prize in European club soccer – the Champions League.

In 2004, he went to England and joined Chelsea. His new club won the Premiership in his very first season in charge.

'I am not the least bit afraid of the future,' Jose Mourinho has said. 'I have great confidence in myself and my knowledge. I know that I can make a difference and that I can win.'

Jose Mourinho is like a guided missile. From a young age, Mourinho had a crystal-clear sense of destiny. Nothing deflects or distracts Jose Mourinho from where he is heading, he is locked into a wavelength of achievement, power and self-determination. Jose Mourinho lives in a 'State of Grace'.

We all know a 'Jose Murinho'. We often don't like them. Perhaps he was the boy at school who was captain of the soccer team and went out with the prettiest girl. She was effortlessly accomplished, elegant, popular and destined for great things. Now he/she lives in the biggest house, drives the best car, has the biggest bank account, goes on the best holidays and always seems to be in the right place at the right time. *People like that are just so damned annoying.*

Jose Mourinho irritates other managers. They hate his posturing, his designer clothes, his smouldering looks, his appetite for confrontation. They long to see him brought down to size, eating humble pie, admitting he's not that special after all. They've got it *the wrong way around.* Instead of sniping and criticising and bitching about Mourinho's achievements, they should be learning to follow his example. And so should you.

Instead of envying the accomplishments of your rich or happy or 'more fortunate' acquaintances, you should be sitting them down and picking their brains. I realise you hate their guts and would rather stick pins in your eyes than give them the satisfaction of doing any such thing but this is not about them. *This is about you.*

Before you pick up the receiver, return briefly to Session 6. What really concerns you about asking for help *is adding to their power by giving away yours.* This is what you would have done in the past. **Now, you won't.** Summon your Generals, marshal your forces and create a battle plan. Then pick up the phone.

Where winning begins

> 'A mind, once stretched by a new idea, never regains its original dimensions.'
>
> OLIVER WENDELL HOLMES

I am already working on my next book. It's called *The 1%*. When I'm not working with sportsmen, executives or making TV shows, I do a great deal of speaking at corporate events or providing after-dinner presentations. The title of one of my speeches is 'The Secrets of Winning'. Accompanied by clips of famous footballers, golfers and rugby stars, I explain how to adapt the psychological techniques employed by international sportsmen and women to achieve success in the corporate arena. The first line of the speech goes like this: 'One per cent of people lead the life of their dreams. Everyone else helps that tiny group to make those dreams come true.'

Dynamic, focused, special people ARE different. They radiate a sense of destiny, a purpose, a *certainty* that enables them to shape their future. Great men and women seem to bend the energy of the world to their will. **This is not an illusion.** *They really do.* There is no magic involved, this is not voodoo or sorcery. If you want to be what they are and have what they have, you had better learn how they do it.

We're almost there:

You know Who You Are.
You know What You Want.

You've drawn up the Plan that will bring it about.
You've got all the Belief that you will need.
The time has come to *Live It.*

Few high achievers know how they succeed. Most put their achievements down to resolve, commitment and a refusal to take 'No' for an answer. It's much more than that. Plenty of hungry, gifted, dedicated individuals set out on the path to achievement. Very few make it. Something extra is needed. This session concentrates on one specific quality – **mindset.** This is the combination of attitudes and responses that sets the greats well and truly apart. It is a way of *being* that will take the structure we've built in this book onto a far higher plane. *This is about making your action plan live!*

Absorb the lessons of this session deeply and carefully. I want you to become a Jose Mourinho – an unstoppable force, a locomotive of intention speeding towards the life you dream of. Nothing gets in the way of Mourinho – or Tiger Woods, or Philip Green or Oprah Winfrey or Steven Spielberg. Nothing should get in your way either.

LEARN FROM 'THE MATERIAL GIRL'
Madonna arrived in New York in the early eighties **with nothing.** She lived in abject poverty for years and survived on supermarket leftovers.

I have boundless admiration for Madonna. She might slap me for saying this, but La Ciccone is not a particularly gifted singer or songwriter or dancer or actress. Today, Madonna is worth an estimated

£150 million, has homes on both sides of the Atlantic and has spent two decades as one of the most famous women in the world.

And it is all down to mindset. Madonna set her mind to realising her dreams. Like Jose Mourinho, she was (and is) a guided missile that nothing could prevent from hitting its target. Friends – those who knew her back when – confirm that Madonna *was exactly the same when she had nothing*. She decided. She chose. She made it happen. Nothing could stop her. *She made up her mind*.

I use Madonna as an example because I don't want to hear 'It's easy for them!' Don't try telling me 'They have/they've got/they were born that way'. No they don't. No they haven't. No they were not. *Lack of God-given talent is no excuse*. **They chose**. Now it's your turn.

The rest of this session is devoted to the mindset of champions; to achieving your deepest, most-longed-for desires – **what I call Magnetic Goals**. I am going to:

a) give you three exercises that will help you to install that mindset

b) recommend two further fundamental shifts of attitude.

My intention is to cement the work we've done, taking the foundations down so deep that nothing, but nothing, can blow you off course. You will enjoy these exercises and thoughts, everyone does. I guarantee you will also enjoy what they do.

The Practice of Intention

Every single morning before I get out of bed, and before I have a shower, eat breakfast and start work, I set out what I 'intend' to achieve. By 'set out', I do **not** mean scratch my head, vaguely remember what's in the diary and think about what I might get away with. I mean that I set out my goals for the day. I have a clear mental image of tasks, meetings, speeches, coaching sessions etc., divided into morning, afternoon and evening. **And I give explicit voice – *I declare out loud* – exactly what I am going to achieve.** Before I get out of bed in the morning, I know a great day lies in store.

These goals might be big or small. For instance, this morning I committed to touching base with three clients, planning a speech I am making later this week and playing cricket with my son. I know I will do all these and more.

Yours might include:

    I intend to get to work on time
    I intend to have a productive team meeting
    I intend to resolve that issue with my colleague
    I intend to enjoy the evening with my partner
    I intend to have a fabulous day

The Practice of Intention will send energy forward and set up your day in the way you want it to pan out. Inject as much *feeling* as you can into the process. Half-hearted feeling creates half-hearted days. Project, ahead of time, exactly what you want to experience.

The process is straightforward:

1. Clear a quiet, *private* space. This will only take a few moments but is not to be rushed. Get up five minutes earlier if necessary. Find somewhere you will not be disturbed.
2. Think about each segment of the day, one at a time. What is going on? What are you doing? What do you want to achieve?
3. It goes without saying that not everything in life gets the mouth watering in anticipation. It doesn't matter. What does matter is *finding something about each task that's worth having.* Take mowing the lawn. Yes, you'd rather be inside with your feet up reading the paper but that's not going to happen. Actually, it just might. *Intend* it. *Intend* to have the lawn mown by 12 o'clock. *Intend* to sit with those brogues on the settee, looking out of your window and admiring your work. *Intend* to feel how good it is to have the rest of the day off.
4. Say it out loud. Go on, don't be shy. No one is listening except me: 'I intend to have the lawn finished by midday and be on the Playstation by ten past twelve.'
5. Fast-forward to a time after the event has happened and *feel.* Allow all the great feelings

of accomplishment (in this case) or pleasure or
satisfaction to flood through your body. Stay
with it for 20 seconds. Feel yourself on that
settee doing nothing at all.

Mowing the lawn is an easy one (especially if you've
got one of those mowers that you sit on). The Practice
of Intention comes into its own where doubts are
harboured.

Put it to the test when your day provides hurdles
you would rather not have to overcome. Be clear
about what it is you intend to have accomplished
and by when. Then fast-forward *to a time after the
event* and savour how good it will *feel* to have got
whatever you want.

A note of caution – *do not use the Practice of
Intention lightly*. Just because you happen to be
working on relatively minor goals that, in the final
analysis, you can take or leave, this does not diminish
the effort required. *All* goals are important. Do you
want it or not? This is your route to the big time –
Magnetic Goals await.

LIVING WITH PURPOSE

Premiership footballers only train for two hours a
day. They turn up at around ten, run round a field,
kick a ball for twenty minutes, lift a few weights and
then head off home. It's all over by half past twelve.
Heaven forbid that their sports psychologist should
suggest they stay behind to work on their minds.

On one particularly tricky job I was making very

slow progress. And I wasn't happy. After a while I couldn't bear it any longer. I called a team meeting and asked the players what they wanted to get out of training. It all went quiet. So, I asked the backroom staff. They didn't have much idea, either. Everyone knew they should do it, so they did. I had my answer. They were simply going through the motions.

I cut to the chase. I demanded to know at the end of each week, how much fitter, stronger, more tactically aware or skilled at communication our squad had become than they were on Monday morning. In other words, *what was the purpose of training?* Embarrassed laughter was the response.

Once the players had left, I sat down with the staff. I challenged them to come up with Process Goals – improvements in speed, skill, stamina and teamwork that could be worked on and *measured* each day. Training would be restructured to ensure that these variables – which would deliver the three necessary match-winning points every Saturday – were the focus of attention all week. *I gave training a purpose.*

Purpose puts our actions in context. Without context, we drift. Without purpose, we are aimless: each day or week or month is just like the last. We bob along without knowing why we are bobbing or what we are bobbing towards.

High achievers tolerate no such bobbing. Outstanding individuals act with purpose in everything that they do. They radiate purpose. Everyone around them can sense their hunger, their palpable quality of momentum.

My clients do not drift and neither will you. Whether

you are performing the most menial of tasks or the most critical, I want you to instil each and every one with real purpose. I want you to bring a quality of deliberation to every aspect of your life. From driving to work to cooking a meal, from playing sport to talking on the phone, *learn to do so with purpose*. The sense of vigour, of energy and of possibility this will give you is awesome.

Easier said than done? Let's take something simple – going to the shops. Millions of us take such trips every day of the week. How can we infuse such a seemingly mundane task with a compelling sense of purpose?

It goes back to the power of WHY. If one of my clients was about to go shopping, I would ask, 'Why are you going?' . . . 'What is your purpose in this shopping?' At first, some of the answers would be hesitant but, gradually, momentum would build: 'I am going shopping because . . .'

It gets me out of the office
It'll give me some much-needed exercise
I enjoy chatting to staff and cashiers
I need to feed my family
I buy nice things for my family
I provide for my loved ones
I make my loved ones happy
Which makes me feel needed
That makes me content
I am fulfilled

Suddenly 'shopping' is not just about shopping. Shopping is about happiness. Shopping delivers fulfilment. How differently do you think that person will anticipate shopping from now on?

I want you to approach every task every day in this manner. Find a sense of purpose in everything you do. Notice how you start to buzz, to tingle, *to relish the approach of each new experience.*

The benefits are exponential. The more purpose you have, the more internal power you generate. The vigour, the self-belief, the sense of possibility this gives you is phenomenal. As purpose expands, you expand too.

As if

This is a game I play with my clients. The rules of 'As if' are simple. I ask them to go inside and imagine that all their wants have come to pass. Opening their eyes, they act 'as if' it was true. They stand, sit, move, breathe, stare, glare, walk, talk, strut and pose as if they had already become that person. The effect is instantaneous. They stand taller, breathe easily, look sharper and speak more clearly.

This is playacting with a purpose. When they leave at the end of our session, I ask them to get on the train with that attitude and take it to work – and into their sport, and into their relationships. What starts out as fun soon gets serious. They find that strangers view them differently. They enjoy levels of respect, acknowledgement and responsibility that previously were well out of reach. They *like* it.

In fact, this is not playacting at all. What they have started to do is build a connection *with their own power*, the power they have only stepped into now and again in the past but always knew was there.

Please try it. What seems strange at first will soon grow familiar, solid, *appropriate*. Start living from this place. It doesn't have to be the whole time – indeed, it won't be. Accept that *solidity* will come and go – and enjoy the feeling of conviction while it lasts. I know, believe me, that there's a lot to remember in this book, and this is one more thing to be added to your list of 'must dos', *BUT* – high achievers *do* live in this place. When I urged you to 'live it' at the start of this chapter, this was the 'it' that I referred to.

If you are living in True Self, the job is half done (more than half!). This is just another layer, another way of adding richness to the texture of the True You.

Children play 'pretend' the whole time. Adults should join in. Daring to imagine all you could be isn't childish at all.

Stick to your goals, regardless

If I have a role model at all, it's Bob Geldof. What I admire so much about Geldof isn't just his infinite compassion or the stunning achievements of Live Aid/Live 8. What I admire about Geldof is he doesn't give a toss.

By saying and doing precisely as he chooses, Geldof has antagonised virtually everyone. He is utterly fearless. This is the man who travelled into the heart of African darkness and assailed Colonel Mengistu, the Ethiopian despot, for putting his war effort before famine relief. He is the personification of my *Dare* philosophy.

Bob Geldof is, at all times, emphatically himself. He refuses to compromise his personality, his beliefs or his style to please the crowd. More to the point, he doesn't give a stuff about the crowd in the first place.

This is one of the chief characteristics of high achievers: they feel no need to secure the admiration or approval of others. What anyone else thinks of them is of limited interest.

Please note that I use the phrase 'limited interest' – which is by no means the same as 'complete disregard'. High achievers understand that results depend on collective effort, that one individual can only accomplish so much on their own. Geldof did not alienate the politicians whose help he would need nor the other performers at Live Aid (well, not all of them).

Most of all, high achievers are in no way influenced by what others may think about their goals. Every single one of them has put up with someone (usually close, often *very* close) telling them to 'forget it'. The strength of character to smile politely and get on with their project is a non-negotiable trait.

High performers are often nonconformist. That nonconformism may be exhibited in what they wear or say or expect or reveal or demand or – and this is the real test – refuse to do. They are often difficult, uncooperative, outrageous, surprising, infuriating, captivating, pigheaded and, quite frankly, a 'pain in the ass'. *We need a lot more like them.*

The Mindset of Champions

One of the outstanding characteristics of 'The 1%' (the people leading the life of their dreams) is their refusal to acknowledge failure. Setbacks are dismissed as either irrelevant or a useful indicator of how to succeed.

By any standards, Thomas Edison was one of the key figures of the twentieth century; but, for many years, the man who figured out how to harness electricity was regarded as a crackpot. He was the original mad genius whose experiments always ended in disaster. Edison was oblivious. Ten thousand experiments went wrong before Edison proved electricity wasn't just one of his ridiculous fantasies. You read that right, *ten thousand*.

His place in history established, the Great Man was asked if he'd ever thought about giving up. 'Not at all,' he said. 'I had to succeed because I ran out of ways to fail.'

At what point would you have given up? I know you probably failed school science exams, but put yourself in Edison's shoes for a few moments. How long would you have given it – 500 experiments? 1000? 2000?

The more important (with all due respect) question is – why didn't *Edison* quit? The great man didn't persist out of mere stubbornness. Though that clearly helped. *Edison persisted because of what he was drawn towards*. He was drawn on by what I have called 'Magnetic Goals'.

Magnetic Goal is destiny. It is the endgame, the achievement, the result. 'The 1%' – that outstandingly successful bunch of Magnetic Goal-scorers – are laser beams in human form. They see, hear, feel, think, believe, taste and *know* their destination. Every cell of their being is *certain* about the realisation of their desires. They don't hope or aspire or wish or try. They *know*. In their minds, in their beings, in their souls, success is a done deal.

Now for *your* endgame – the scoring of your Magnetic Goals. All we have done so far together in this book is about arriving in this place. Do you really want what you say you want or are you lying to yourself? Because you *can* have it. My work with 'The 1%' proves it. Be careful what you wish for because *it is going to come true*.

Finding your own Magnetic Goal

- Get yourself a chair and sit down. Make sure you won't be disturbed for 60 seconds. That's all it takes.
- Fast-forward to the **achievement** of your goals. You know your goals by now – inside out, I hope. If you don't, if there is one shred of extra clarity needed, go back and get it.
- Pick a goal – a big one, preferably; one that gets all your juices flowing simultaneously.
- Picture it. You've got it! It's happened! You've won! You've made it! You've done it! Feels good doesn't it? 'Feels good' is nothing like 'good' enough; I want it to feel *fabulous, sensational, phenomenal*. Turn up the emotion. Your joy and

wonder and feelings of ecstasy must be completely overpowering. It's got to be almost more than you can bear. I want these emotions to resonate so strongly through every inch of your essence that – and this is the biggie – *they are still there after you've opened your eyes*. Choose your moment. Stay with those sensations for at least 30 seconds (big dreams take no longer than small ones) then slowly (slowly!) come back into the room. Can you still feel it? The emotion may have slightly diminished but *it should still remind you of the specific desire you've just 'achieved'*. Each desire carries with it a different emotion.

Do this for each of your goals in turn. Twice per week is ample. If you have a goal list of seven items, this exercise will take up precisely two minutes of your day.

And it works. Boy, does it work. Sometimes, right away.

Set yourself up for success

Jean is a self-employed marketing genius. We've known each other for ten years and she's always had more work than she can possibly handle. We like to meet in Selfridges Coffee Shop for a cake and a natter (I eat, she talks). Unusually, Jean was worried. Her father had died a few months earlier and work had been quiet ever since. Could I help?

Absolutely. I explained to Jean how the emotional 'down' that can follow the death of a parent will often seep into other areas. Live in a low place and the virus of 'low' will spread where it definitely is not meant to go.

Jean took a gulp of mocha and closed her eyes. We projected forward ten days. I told her the phone was ringing. On the other end of the line was a client offering Jean two big contracts. I encouraged Jean to feel excited, delighted, relieved. She immediately felt better and promised to repeat the exercise on the train home.

Jean rang my mobile *four* days later. The call had come but it was three contracts not two. Could I please get it right next time? I said I'd try.

What 'The 1%' know is this – **success is a decision that is made in advance.** You have got to make up your mind. Set your mind and your mind is set. *Know* it will happen. No doubts, no fears, no second-guesses. Restrain the impulse to 'worry' because your desire hasn't come about yet. Worry, as I said at the start of this session, is a 'don't want'.

Practising this exercise will turn YOU into a guided missile. Nothing can stand in the way of your desires.

So choose your goal with care. Be careful what you wish for. You can have it. You will have it. You have learned how to DARE.

Session Summary

1. Practise intention before you get out of bed in the morning. Don't rush. Send out precisely what you want to get back.

2. Drifting is such an ingrained part of most people's behaviour that they don't even know they are lost. Find a purpose in everything that you do.

3. Whose approval do you want? Are they a part of 'The 1%'? High achievers need approval from no one.

4. Adopt the mindset of champions. Tune into and turn *up* your Magnetic Goals.

You Can Have It All

One of the most remarkable films of recent years has precisely the kind of title that would put you off seeing it. *What the Bleep Do We Know!?* (2004) is about quantum physics (another good reason, you might think, for giving this one a wide berth). I thought so, too, until I took a call from my brother Roger. 'What are you doing this evening?' he inquired – not, as it turned out, that he was in the least bit interested. 'Never mind,' he said, before I could even get a word in. 'We're going to the cinema.'

I muttered and grumbled about being too busy and having other plans but Roger turned up at 8 p.m. on the dot. Resistance was clearly futile so I decided to inject some fun into the evening by eating my way through a box of Maltesers.

I didn't even open the cellophane. From first frame to last, *What the Bleep Do We Know!?* was gripping. Much much *much* more to the point, it turned out to be a cinematic representation of the work I'd been doing for years.

The film was a blend of drama and talking heads. The talking heads included several of the world's most learned thinkers and physicists. What they were talking about was the new model of science – a *model that proclaims* **what happens within a human being determines what happens outside.** No wonder Roger had told me to drop everything.

Without spoiling the movie (please see it or buy it or rent it on DVD), let me share a few highlights. Every second, 400 billion bits of information pass through our brains. *400 billion!!!* Our conscious minds are only capable of processing 2000 bits of data. *So we choose what we process. We choose what's familiar.* We filter out everything that doesn't fit our existing view of the world.

One of the most dramatic examples of this phenomenon occurred when Christopher Columbus arrived on American soil. The land was occupied by Native Indians who had never seen a ship. 'Ship' was not a concept they had any way of comprehending. Columbus's boat was a few hundred yards from the shoreline **and they couldn't see it.** The Indians filtered out the information that didn't conform to their view of the world. It was only when the shaman of the tribe (someone they knew and could trust) told them there was a strange new object in the water that the Indians were able to see what had been there all along.

The movie's next important point is that the human brain makes sense of the world by creating neuronets. A neuronet is a connection of nerve cells. Each time 'something' happens (love, anger, regret, disappointment), these nerve ends interpret such events by joining together to create a link. That link becomes our 'explanation' of 'how life is'. Our neuronets are our reality.

So what? Here's what – neuronets are not permanent.

If things don't turn out the way we anticipate (i.e. according to the structure of our neuronet), we provide ourselves with a new 'explanation'. **The nerve cells break apart and new neuronets are formed.** We have changed! We are different! We have evolved. And all this is initiated by thought.

Roger had to restrain me from jumping out of my seat. It was instantly apparent to me (as I hope it is to you) that high achievers and victims must have entirely different neuronet connections. The links we establish are conditioned by our view of the world. If that view changes, so do we.

This is why my work is so effective. Life coaches help their clients to create new connections (i.e. neuronets) – and therefore lives – that serve their needs. And there, up on the screen, was the proof.

The conclusion reached by *What the Bleep . . .* scientists is that ***thought is the most powerful force in the universe.*** Human beings must stop thinking in terms of 'what is' and think instead of 'what can be'.

Remember Heisenberg's Theory from Session 4 – those particles that moved depending on the nature of the observer? If you accept your world is fixed (and that I've just made all that stuff up about neuronets), you can do little to affect your destiny. In which case, good luck and have a nice life. However, according to this new scientific model, the world is made up of endless possibilities. All we have to do is *choose*.

I talked in our last session about purpose. At some time or another, you must have wondered about yours. *What the Bleep Do We Know!?* concludes that **every**

single one of us is a God in the Making and that our purpose on earth is to develop our gifts of intention by learning how to be effective creators. This is exactly what I have been preaching for years. If anyone had tried telling me a decade ago that we could all have exactly what we wanted, I would have responded with considerable scorn. Or a kick in the crotch. But we can. *You can*. Absolutely anything.

We have already covered some of the reasons why most people don't: they have no idea what they want – even less who they are, they don't believe they can have it, they are surrounded by people telling them they can't and wouldn't know how to start even if they did. In the face of such overwhelming odds, it's no wonder that so few succeed.

You should, by now, have cleared all those hurdles. I believe you are ready to achieve your goals and I hope you do, too. This session reveals why long-standing limitations need no longer apply. Casting them aside *is imperative*.

What has gone before has no bearing on what can be. You are where you are because of where you have been and how you have been and what you believed. Let it go, let it *all* go. It hasn't worked, it doesn't serve you and it transparently never will. Have the courage to reinterpret your world view. Examine the fresh evidence and create new neuronet connections. Be, at last, all that you can be, all that you want to be, all that you always were. No one except you was stopping you in the first place.

What you think is what you get

What the Bleep . . . reinforces several of the points I covered in Session 7. To recap very briefly, human beings are electromagnetic creatures. Like all electro-magnetic objects, we employ wavelengths. Emotions are emitted on various, but very distinct, electromagnetic wavelengths. The wavelength of optimism is entirely different to the wavelength of despair. The wavelength of love bears no relation to the wavelength of hate. Are you with me so far? Different emotions, distinct wavelengths.

Why do you care? Because one emotion is magnetically attracted to others on the same wavelength. People who are happy get happiness back. People who are wretched get wretchedness back. They attract emotions on the same wavelength! *What you think is what you get.*

I am making no judgements. One kind of thinking is not necessarily good and another is not necessarily bad. What matters is what do you want? And are you thinking in a way that will bring it to fruition?

At a subconscious level, high achievers have always known this. They do not indulge in low-frequency (i.e. depressive) thought because like attracts like – *and it is highly indulgent.*

Where we go wrong

I need you to understand the scale of the illness afflicting society. In order to join 'The 1%', you need to know how the 99% think.

Let me be blunt (I know, *that* makes a change). Virtually everyone you know – and ever have known and ever will know – spends their entire life obsessing about what they absolutely, positively, Dear Lord please help me, DO NOT want to happen. As an example:

- I do not want to get ill
- I do not want to get fired
- I do not want to write off my car
- Or get a parking ticket
- Or lose my friends
- That goes for my money
- And my mobile
- Or fall victim to a terrorist attack
- Or fall out with my kids
- Have a miserable Xmas
- Get divorced
- Get married
- Lose my teeth
- Lose my hair

A lot of depressed people walk through my door. They tell me that everything is going wrong, that everyone is doing better than them, that everyone has more than they do, that life is unfair and 'Why does it always happen to me?' It isn't. It doesn't. It never did. There is no 'it'. 'It' is not happening to them. *They are doing 'it' to themselves.*

A word for Worry Bears. You have my sympathy. At some level you 'believe' that if you worry about something for long enough, that will reduce the odds of it happening; that serving your penance in advance offsets the need for the damage itself. *Wrong way round! Thinking about what you don't want to happen is exactly how it does*. Wavelengths again. No way round.

Substitute anything you like for worry. If you want to stay in debt, focus on having no money. If you don't want to lose your job, think about how awful it would be if you did. On the other hand, you could do precisely the opposite.

The power of thought in action

Football supporters exert a massive influence on the games they attend. If fans want their team to win more often – and they keep telling me that they do – they will have to learn a new way to support them. Two historic games drive the point home.

In 2004, England met France in a group match at the European Championships. This was a true clash of the titans; arguably the strongest teams in the entire tournament had drawn each other in the very first game. England took the lead just before half-time. With one minute of normal time remaining, they were still ahead.

England lost. France equalised in the 90th minute and added a penalty in time added on. England had snatched defeat from the jaws of victory. A nation was stunned. How on earth had it happened?

I was intrigued. France had hardly ever looked like scoring, yet the match was turned on its head in an instant. Could this be about more than 22 men kicking a ball?

I spent several days afterwards talking to people who had been at, or were watching, the game at home. Many observed a 'strange thing happening but weren't too sure how to explain it'. (Always one of my favourite sentences!)

I started piecing the facts together. The atmosphere in the stadium had changed once England had scored. An initial sense of anxiety among England fans (France were the tournament favourites) was replaced by growing levels of confidence that *were transmitted to the players on the pitch*.

With five minutes to go, tension re-emerged. All over the ground, the thinking changed from 'We might actually win' to 'Please, *please* hang on'. Anyone thinking about 'hanging on' is focused on what they don't want to happen (e.g. losing). That focus *was transmitted to the players*. England lost.

Twelve months later, Liverpool played AC Milan in the final of the Champions League. At half-time, Liverpool were 3–0 down and the game was all but over. Here is an extract from a report in *The Times* next day, filed by a writer standing on the terraces:

'There was a moment at half-time when everything changed. Someone started to sing "You'll Never Walk Alone" [the anthem of Liverpool FC] and we rose as one from our disappointment and pledged allegiance. It didn't matter that we were three down . . . and, as the song finished, we began to chant another: "We're going to win 4–3".'

The focus of the fans had switched from 'What we don't want' (losing) to 'What we do' (getting back in the game). That attitude *was transmitted to the players on the pitch*.

When Liverpool's captain, Steven Gerrard, scored to make it 3–1, the atmosphere changed again. Now the focus was on *opportunity*. Liverpool went on to equalise and win on penalties – arguably the greatest comeback in the history of the game.

After the match, Steven Gerrard would pay tribute to his side's 'twelfth man' on the terraces. Quite right, too. While prime responsibility was clearly down to the players, Gerrard recognised the very real link between what happened on the terraces and the result. It was greater than he could possibly have appreciated. On that night in Istanbul, the collective desire of Liverpool supporters transformed the performance of their side. England, by contrast, had been brought down by the fear of their travelling fans.

Pragmatists may scoff (and football is full of them) but supporters play a fundamental role in determining the fate of their teams. I call it 'The Golden Triangle'; it links a team, a city (or country) and its fans. If they are serious about getting what they want, teams and their supporters need to learn how to win.

What can I do?

You should already be doing it! This is where everything in this book comes together. Simply focus on what you *do* want to happen, and whatever it is you want to achieve, and then return to the Magnetic Goals exercise from our last session.

Project yourself forward to a time when your desire has already materialised. Turn the emotional dial up as high as you can and make it glow in every cell of your being. Be patient, stay alert. Your desires are on their way and will arrive in their own time. Keep an eye out for small hints and clues – or signs that they are starting to materialise. Most desires manifest themselves in a way that never would have occurred to the manifestor. No great surprise, there. If the individual had known what to do, he/she would already have done it.

Bringing desires into being is classic right-brain activity. It is not logical, it is not linear. Don't expect it to 'make sense'. In fact, do not expect anything. Be silent, be ready, be *certain*. It is already approaching.

The Holy Grail – Abundance

Abundance is my favourite word. It used to be chocolate but then I found something better. The *Collins Oxford Dictionary* describes abundance as: 1. a copious supply, great amount. 2. fullness or benevolence – e.g. *from the abundance of my heart*. I would go further. Abundance, to my way of thinking, carries a quality of boundlessness. It is something that cannot run out and will not dry up no matter how much is used or consumed.

One of the questions I sometimes ask clients (especially those whose goals are a tad materialistic) is this:

If I gave you the choice between . . .

   a)   £10 million or
   b)   fulfilling your destiny

. . . which would you pick?

Your turn. Think carefully. You don't want to feel embarrassed midway through the next sentence.

The number that choose a) is depressing. They might as well have 'Show Me the Money' tattooed across their foreheads. £10 million might buy you a lot of cars, houses, holidays, plastic surgery etc. – OK, it *will* buy you a lot of cars, houses etc. – but *it is finite*! (Yes, I have heard of compound interest but let's not get smart.) One day it *will* run out. Yes, really – unless you live like a miser, which is hardly abundant.

I am going to show you how real abundance is achieved. Nowhere in print has this material appeared before. It is emphatically, unequivocally at the leading edge of human thought.

Abundance comes in ten thousand guises. Abundance isn't just about money but includes love, health, environment and opportunity. The method that I am going to describe works with them all. Let me begin with an example of my own.

THE MUSIC OF ABUNDANCE
As you may recall from the introduction to this book, I was a rock critic for many years. I still write occasion-

ally for one or two newspapers. I bought my first record when I was five. ('Have I The Right?' by the Honeycombs, since you ask.) I was *obsessed* with music, particularly the Beatles. I spent all my pocket money on their records, posters and fan-club magazines. I was buying *Melody Maker* at seven. I was a walking encyclopaedia of pop trivia!

This was devotion, pure and simple. As I got older, and I don't care how melodramatic this sounds, music – many times – gave me a reason to live. I looked forward, for months in advance, to seeing and hearing the latest bands. I counted the days until certain albums came out.

One of the main privileges of being a rock critic is that you get all the latest albums for nothing. I was like a kid in the world's biggest toy shop. At one time, I must have had 5,000 albums. I used to place the latest arrivals around the room so I could see them when I walked in. They were a constant reminder of how lucky I was. I never left them piled in a heap. I treated them lovingly. I looked after each one. I *treasured* those records.

And they kept coming. Day after day would bring more by post or courier. I started giving away those I didn't particularly appreciate to people who would. I was careful (I cared that much) to ensure they went to a good home.

I was living in a state of abundance. The more I gave away, the more I received. Albums started arriving without my even asking for them. You can't get more abundant than that. Whatever I wanted, I got.

I also mentioned my stint as a movie critic. Once I was ensconced as the movie correspondent of a national newspaper, I told my wife that I aimed to become the new Barry Norman. That still puzzles her today. 'You usually get what you want,' she reminded me recently. 'What happened there?'

What happened was something totally unexpected. After a few weeks of watching movies all day, I found I didn't enjoy it. I was so sure I would; *I was absolutely certain.* But as the opening credits rolled on the third film of yet another day spent in the darkness, I gave vent to a sigh and wished I was outside.

My connection with movies turned out to be far weaker than my relationship with music. There wasn't the same passion, the same regard, the same *adoration*. Many years later, I realised it was this distinction that could unlock the door to abundance. Let me do that for you now.

THE NATURE OF ABUNDANCE

What do you want, at this moment, that you don't have? Money, probably. That's OK, it usually is. We'll be coming to money very soon. Of course, it could be one of many things. You could be yearning for a new car, a new house or to be in a loving relationship.

What you want is *over there*. You are over here and it is over there. It is distant. It is remote. *It is cold.*

What we want and we don't have, *is cold.* What we want and we don't have – in its natural state – *is frozen.* When I ask clients to think about their desires, they often tell me they are a long way away, or packed in a box, or airless or arid or threatening. Fundamentally, *they are cold – always cold.* Our task is to *warm them up*. In order to have whatever you want, those desires need to be converted into a living, breathing, sentient intelligence.

Abudance is a resonant state. It resonates with flow and serendipity and pure possibility. It is not desperate or grasping or selfish or needy. It is guided by reverence. Most of all, it is *a two-way relationship*. My relationship with music was entirely different (specifically warmer) than my feelings towards films. You have to change the way you relate to your dreams.

CONDITIONS FOR ABUNDANCE

It would be foolhardy for me to declare that there exists a definitive template for creating abundance. Neverthless, the following conditions create the best possible environment in which abundance is able to flourish.

1. *Dedication* I like to use the metaphor of a fruit machine (this is not an invitation to gamble!). If you put a handful of coins into a fruit machine, your return will almost certainly be minimal. You need to pick up on the cadences and rhythms of the machine. Experienced players understand that you may have to stand there for hours. Perseverance is essential.

I think of our dreams as feminine. They need to be wooed, to be courted. They must know you are serious. Don't be too forward or impatient. You won't get a kiss on the first date, and a one-night stand is out of the question.

It is the same with abundance. Your desires are not going to drop into your lap (or fall into your arms) on

Day 1. You have to persevere. You have to be ardent, to be patient, to be true. You have to show some commitment.

2. *Service* What will you do with your desires when you get them? If they are purely for personal gain or exploitation, you may spend a long time waiting. This is why those who chase money for its own sake let it slip through their fingers. What you want, when it comes, is, in a very real sense, *giving itself to you*. It has every right to expect that it will be taken care of and looked after.

Books are a perfect example. Collectors of books care deeply about their libraries. They handle the covers gently and regularly clean off the dust. They file their books in a carefully chosen order. They don't stint on bookmarks. They most definitely don't leave books lying around for the Alsatian to chew. Book-lovers revere their collections. To such people, books are not objects – objects are cold. Book lovers invest their collections with warmth.

3. *Devotion* Let's go back to my records. I would never have attracted all that music if I'd just wanted it to impress other people, or have something 'nice' on the sideboard or been 'quite interested' in rock. Devotion is an absolute prerequisite of abundance. If you want a self-replenishing wardrobe full of gorgeous clothes, a passing interest in fashion won't do. Attitude – your attitude – has to be right. Mere interest won't do it. You must be *enraptured*.

4. *Understanding* All right, you've waited long enough, let's talk about money. What do you **know** about money? Do not confuse what you **think** about money (i.e. 'I never have enough, it's hard to find, slips through my fingers') with what you truly, genuinely, deeply **know** about money. I am not sticking my neck out one little bit when I suggest *you know nothing about money.*

Whenever clients ask me to help realise any kind of desire, I set them a task. I challenge them to find out all they can about the object of their desire. I tell them to get under its skin. For example, if what they want is money, I ask them to find out the answers to these questions:

a) What were the origins of money?
b) When was it invented? By whom? Where? Why?
c) What other forms of currency exist?
d) How did notes and coins come about?
e) What is Forex?
f) What is ERM? How does it work?
g) What really happened on Black Wednesday?
h) What are the latest trends in the currency markets?
i) Are interest rates going up or down?
j) Will plastic eventually replace legal tender?
k) What is the future of money?

I challenge them to arrive at our next session and hand me a project. As part of that project, I want them to read the autobiography of someone who has flourished in the financial arena – Richard Branson, perhaps. I also invite them to read Napoleon Hill's book, *Think and Grow Rich*, one of the classic tomes on abundance.

The outcome of such research is a very different attitude towards money. Next time we meet, such clients are fascinated, absorbed and invigorated *by the subject itself* (instead of purely fixated on their want). They understand the hows and whys of money, its ups and its downs. That knowledge, and the perspective it allows, enables them to develop a new relationship with money. This relationship is no longer founded upon fear (of not having) – information has taught them there is *nothing* to be afraid of. Their new relationship is built on respect and understanding.

For the first time in their lives, they have a mature relationship with money. They realise that money is an energy just like any other energy and can be blocked or encouraged in just the same way. Instead of pleading or longing or begging for something beyond their comprehension, they can, at last, bring a clear-sighted, level-headed approach to the job of attainment.

CLIMB THE STAIRCASE TO ABUNDANCE
Here is my suggested five-step path to abundance. Each step leads on naturally from the one before. There should be – *there must be* – a heightening of emotion as you move from Step 1 to Step 5.

1. **Interest:** What catches your attention? What intrigues you? What would you like to know more about?
2. **Curiosity:** Discover, investigate, learn, self-educate.
3. **Engagement:** You are locked on to your desire. It has your attention, your energy, your commitment. Keep going.
4. **Absorption:** You are immersed. Your desire resonates with your True Self.
5. **Devotion:** You are – entirely in accordance with your wishes – in the service of your desire.

YOUR CUP RUNNETH OVER

One of my favourite traditions is widely practised in Arabic homes. It is the practice of offering guests anything they like in the house (except the wife – that's Eskimos). This is the ultimate practice of abundance. This is flow in action.

I know I've said this before but:

If you want money, be charitable
If you want kindness, be compassionate
If you want contentment, make others happy
If you want love, give as much as you can

You get the drift. *Abundance is an energy. And you are the generator.*

Session Summary

1. The latest scientific thinking strongly indicates that our life's purpose is to develop our gifts of intention. You are nothing less than a God in the flesh.
2. How many people do you know who are constantly moaning? What do they attract? Avoid dwelling in 'What I Don't Want'.
3. Create the conditions for abundance in your life – dedication, devotion, service, understanding.
4. Research your heart's desires. Information is priceless.
5. Abundance is an energy. Keep it moving.

A Beginning – Not An End

'Those who will not reason, are bigots, those who cannot are fools, and those who dare not are slaves.'

LORD BYRON

'You can't turn back the clock. But you can wind it up again.'

BONNIE PRUDDEN (fitness trainer and author)

My clients are always surprised when I bid them 'Au revoir'. One or two even take it personally. I gently point out that, much as I would *love* to keep seeing them, and yes they can (and should) return for a top-up visit in 3 to 6 months' time, it is my firm conviction that life coaching should have a clear exit point: 10–12 sessions is heaps. Coaches are not, and should never allow themselves to become, crutches for their clients. Anyone who has 'needed' (or been told they need) to keep coming for years should ask my kids' favourite question: 'Are we nearly there yet?'

If you are thinking about working with a coach, please be careful. For obvious reasons, I am a firm believer in coaching – transformation can be dramatic and lasting – but please take the time to locate one who has the depth of expertise you require. Ask around. Find out whom they have worked with; try and collect endorsements from satisfied clients. If they don't have any, you may wonder why.

How can you tell a good coach from a bad one? Here are a few pointers:

- A skilled coach will (initially, at least) do more listening than talking.
- A good coach will know just the right questions to ask.
- A good coach (and this is the big one) will often say the very last thing a client wants to hear.

Anyone that I work with is left in no doubt that they will be standing on their own two feet when we're done. This is the position you should find yourself in now – assuming, of course, you have kept your end of our bargain. If you have diligently followed the exercises and taken stock of the insights you've gleaned, I've no doubt that you are. If you have simply read through the text from cover to cover in the hope that transformation would occur by some magical process of osmosis, I have no doubt that you are not.

Our work is almost done

Before we part, I want you to look back. Take a few moments to reflect, to *luxuriate*, to soak up all the dramatic, unbelievable (you would *not* have believed it was possible!) progress you have made.

Look back (with compassion, please):

- On the you that first picked up this book.
- On the diminished you that was stuck in False Self.
- On the disempowered you that was stripped of self-belief.
- On the demoralised you that had no idea what you wanted.
- On the you that was confused and frustrated and angry and desperate.

That you is a memory. That you has vanished. That you has *gone*.

This is how far you have come. It has been an epic journey, one that I sincerely hope will mark a turning point in your life.

Where to, now?

In Session 3, I talked about celebrating your triumphs. This, by any standards, is a big one. Please, stop for a moment and *truly appreciate what you have done for yourself. Accept* the courage it took to buy this book, *recognise* the dedication you showed when completing all the exercises, *realise* that you did so despite the fact it was exhausting, time-consuming and, let's face it, there were a thousand other things you would rather have been doing.

But you've made it. Remember my definition of self-confidence – a state of trust between 'you' and 'you'. This is what it feels like. This is what it gives you – an entirely new platform from which to take on the world.

Saying goodbye is part of the process. In a strange way, I look forward to saying goodbye to clients because it means they are ready. It means they no longer need me. It means they have got what they came for. I hope you have, too.

This is where I get my fulfilment: seeing the glint of ambition back in the eyes of my clients; watching them bounce out of the room with purpose in their step; knowing that they will be fine on their own.

You don't need me any more, either. You have what you need. *You have yourself.*

You are an adult. You are a realist. You know that life won't always be plain sailing. You don't expect that everything will always go according to plan. When problems arise, come back to this book. Each and every process bears repetition: find the exercise that will help you get over this strictly temporary hurdle. Problems are fine. *You can cope.*

Truth or Dare? – both, actually

This is a beginning, not an end. What you have created is a springboard, *a launching pad*. What you now have is absolute, pure and simple opportunity. *You are operating on a higher plane.* Life is so much richer up here; more exciting, more meaningful and more contented. This is a place of joy, of hope, of wonder, of expectation, of excitement.

This is my final challenge, one last DARE from me

to you. *Keep going. Never stop!* Keep pushing, keep climbing, keep s-t-r-e-t-c-h-i-n-g. You have what you need to go **much** higher still.

Keep daring. Let the end of this book be the start of your journey. Hold true to yourself and reach for your dreams. Don't stop until they are yours.